EASY PIANO

the best of hosanna! music®

ISBN 0-634-07384-2

HAL•LEONARD®
CORPORATION
7777 W. BLUEMOUND RD. P.O. BOX 13819 MILWAUKEE, WI 53213

Visit Hal Leonard Online at
**www.halleonard.com**

# ANCIENT OF DAYS

Words and Music by GARY SADLER
and JAMIE HARVILL

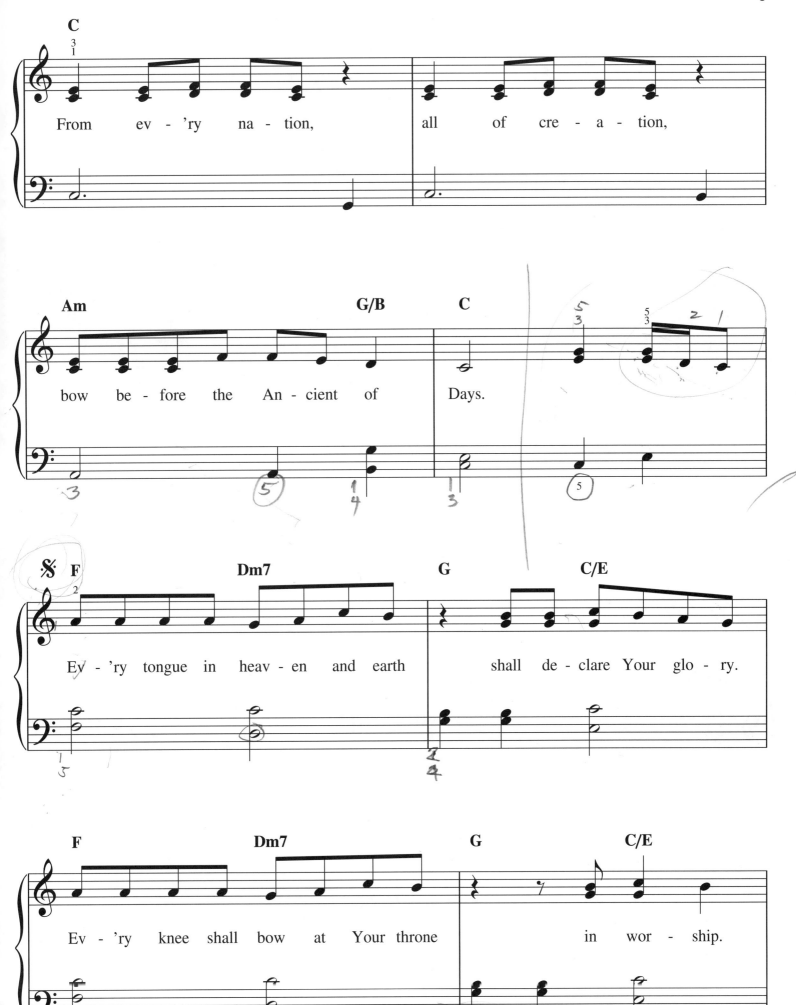

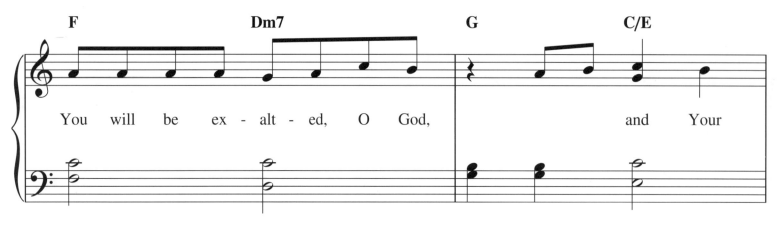

You will be ex - alt - ed, O God,      and  Your

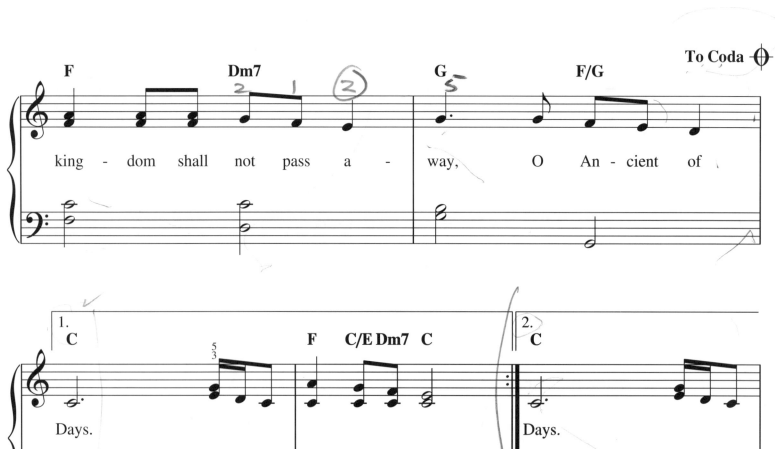

king - dom shall not pass a - way,  O An - cient of

1. Days.

2. Days.

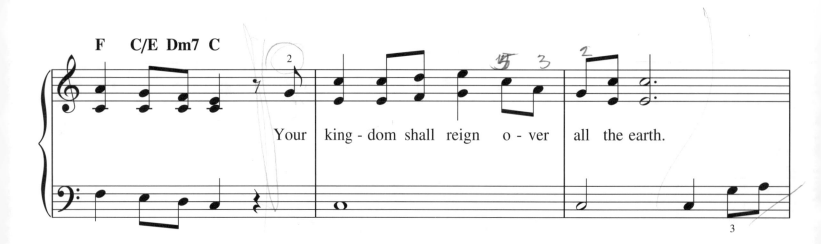

Your king - dom shall reign o - ver all the earth.

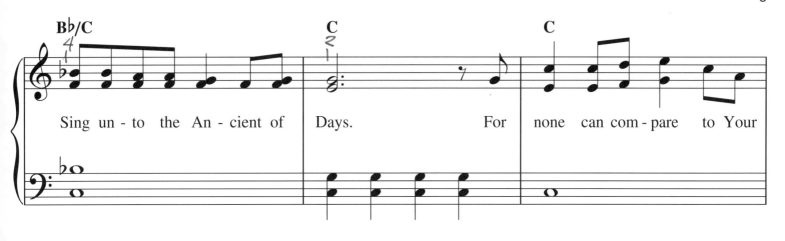

Sing un - to the An - cient of Days. For none can com - pare to Your

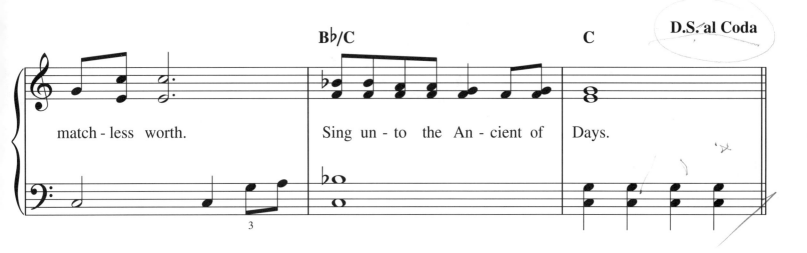

**D.S. al Coda**

match - less worth. Sing un - to the An - cient of Days.

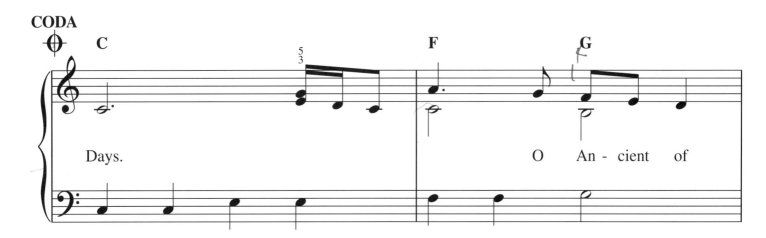

**CODA**

Days. O An - cient of

Days. O An - cient of Days.

# AWESOME GOD

Words and Music by
RICH MULLINS

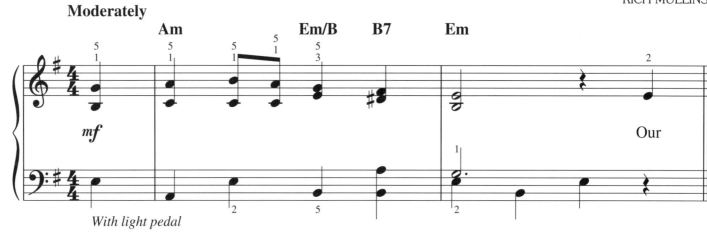

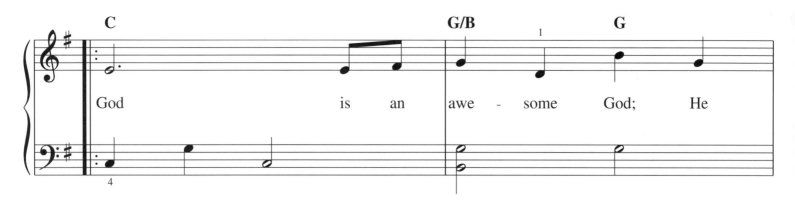

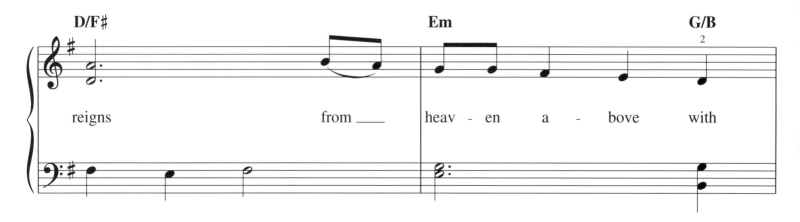

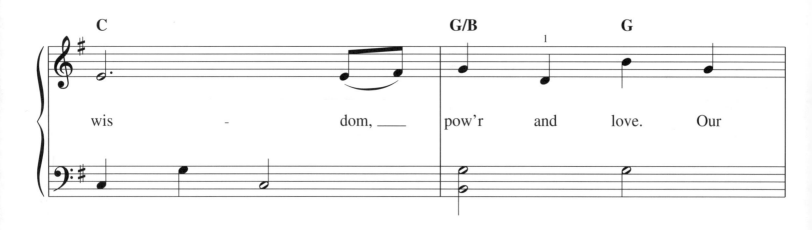

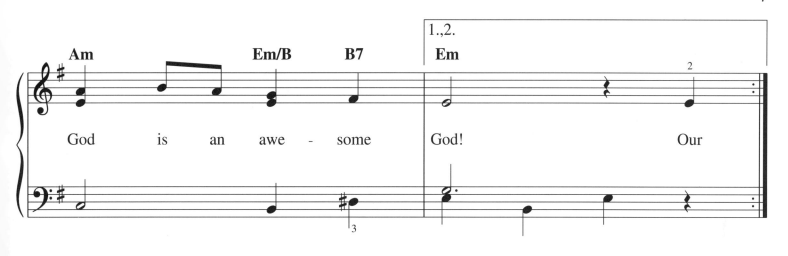

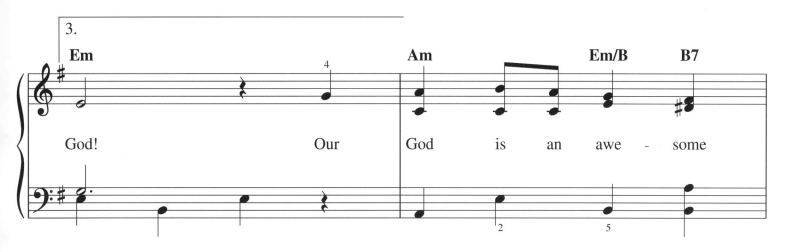

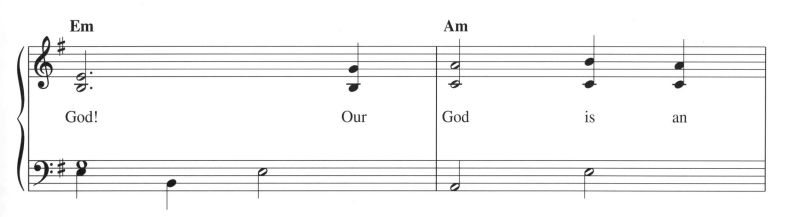

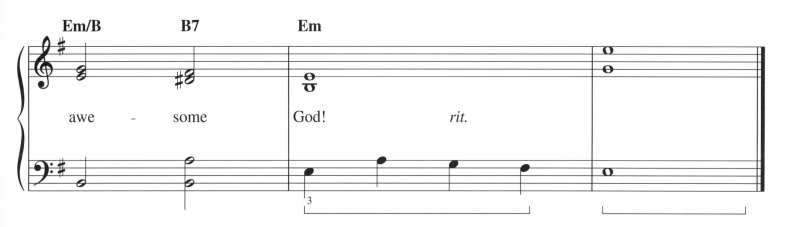

# AWESOME IN THIS PLACE

Words and Music by
DAVID BILLINGTON

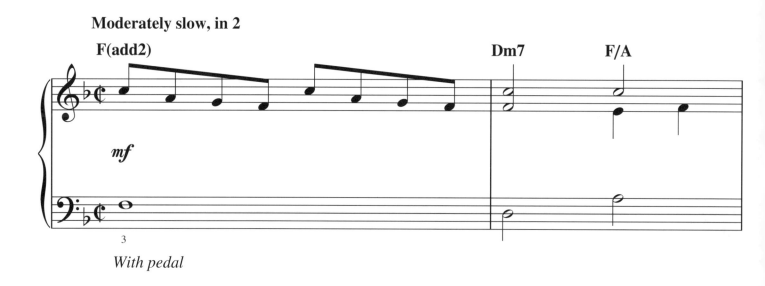

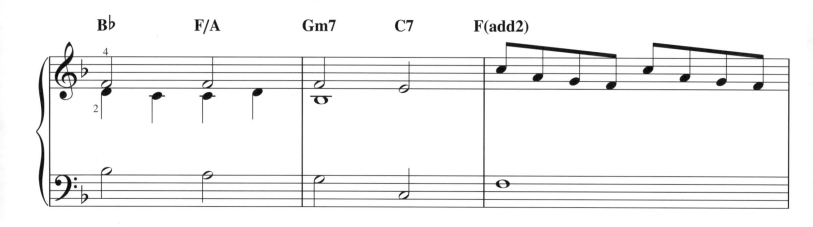

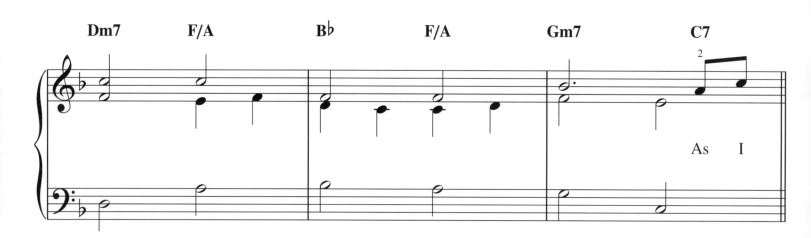

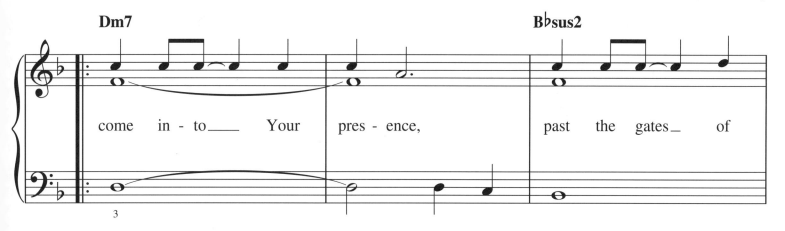

come in - to\_\_\_ Your pres - ence, past the gates\_ of

praise, in - to Your sanc - tu - ar - y, till we're

stand - ing face\_ to face,\_\_\_ I look up - on Your

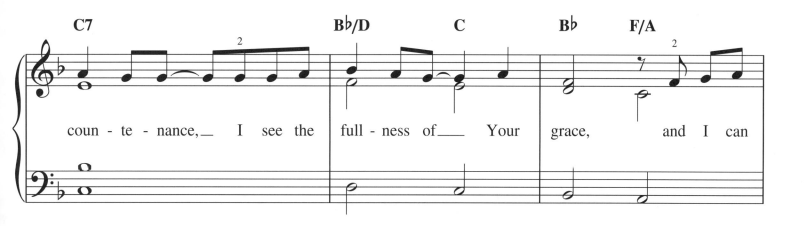

coun - te - nance,\_ I see the full - ness of\_ Your grace, and I can

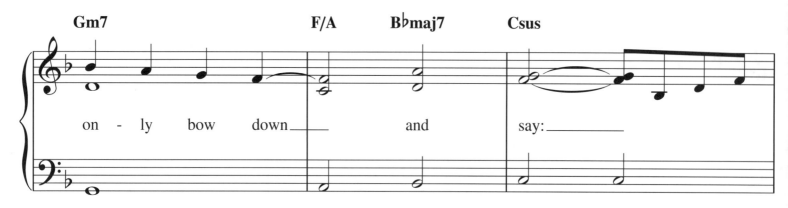

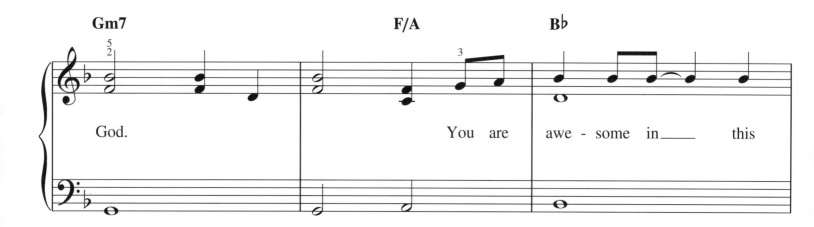

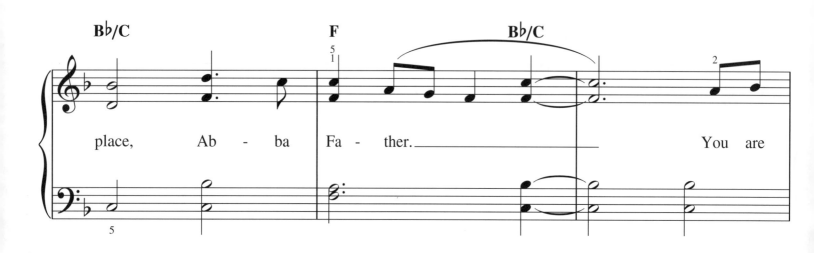

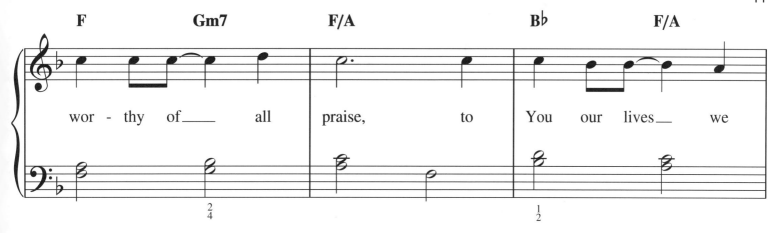

wor - thy of\_\_\_ all praise, to You our lives\_\_ we

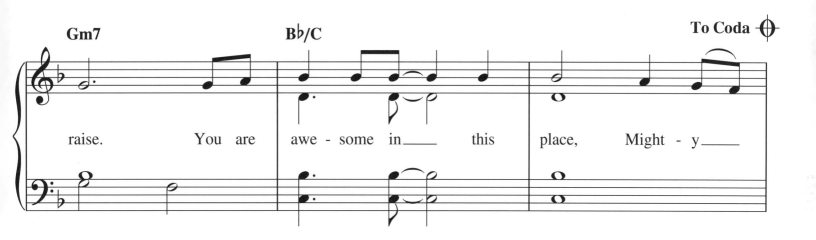

raise. You are awe - some in\_\_\_ this place, Might - y\_\_\_

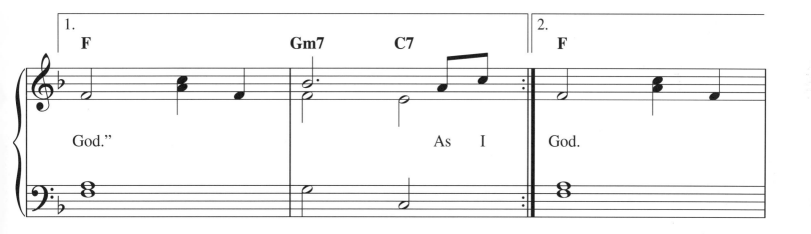

God." As I God.

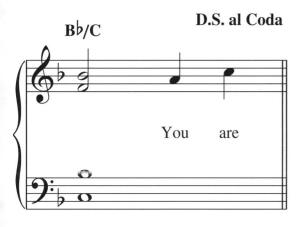

You are

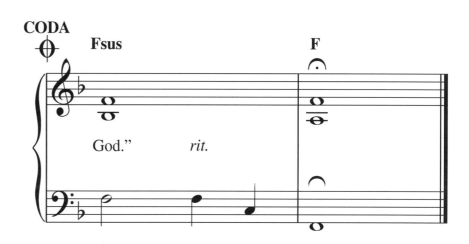

God." *rit.*

# BLESSED BE THE LORD GOD ALMIGHTY

Words and Music by
BOB FITTS

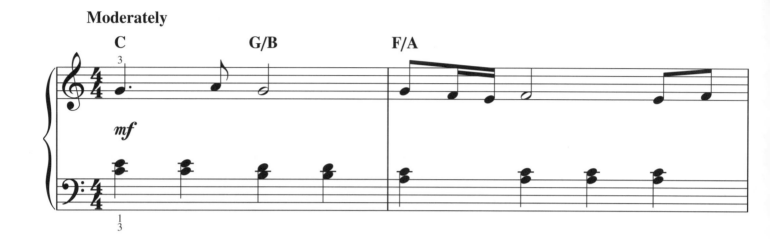

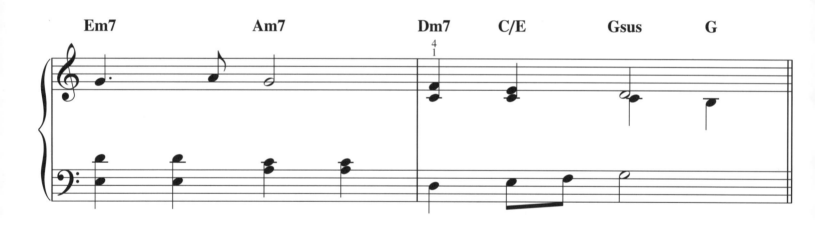

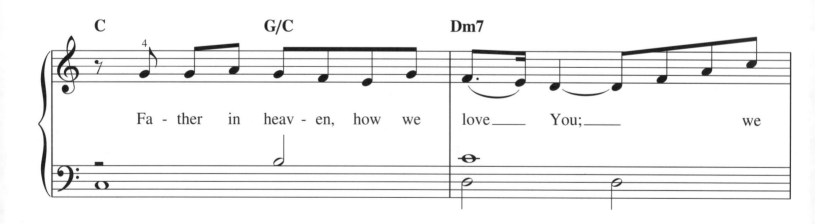

Fa- ther in heav- en, how we love_ You;_ we

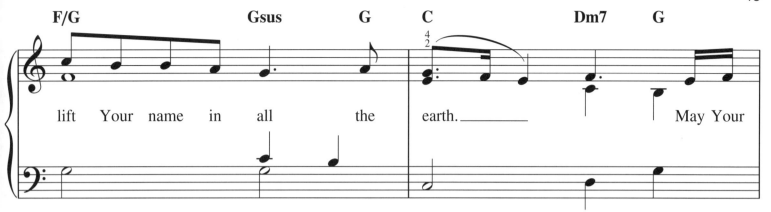

lift Your name in all the earth._____ May Your

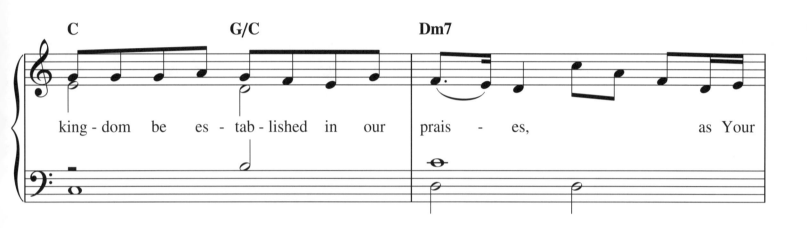

king - dom be es - tab - lished in our prais - es, as Your

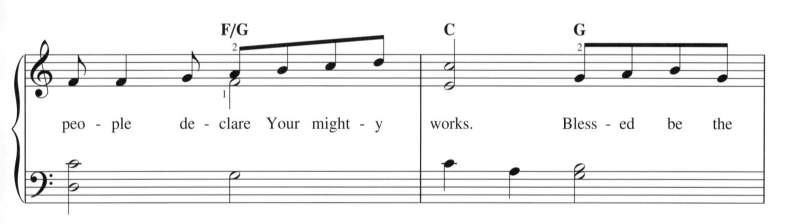

peo - ple de - clare Your might - y works. Bless - ed be the

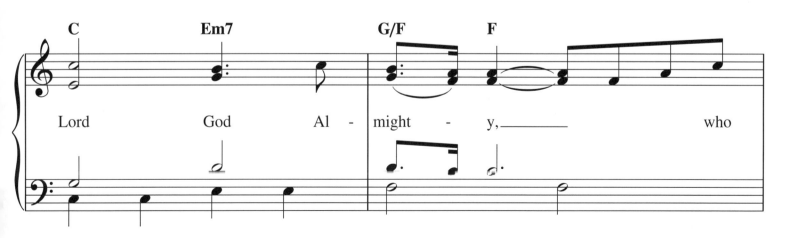

Lord God Al - might - y,_____ who

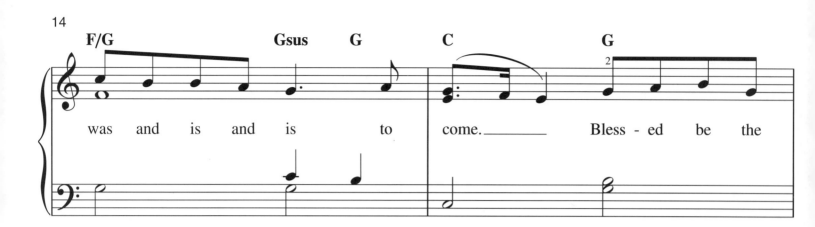

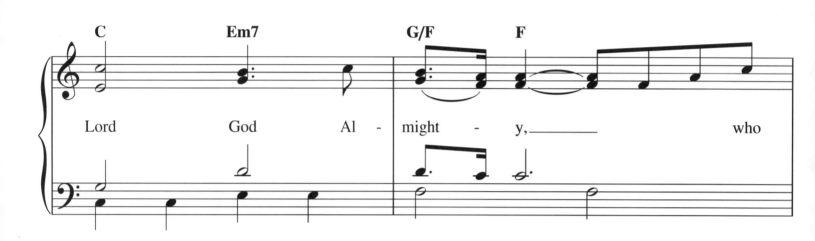

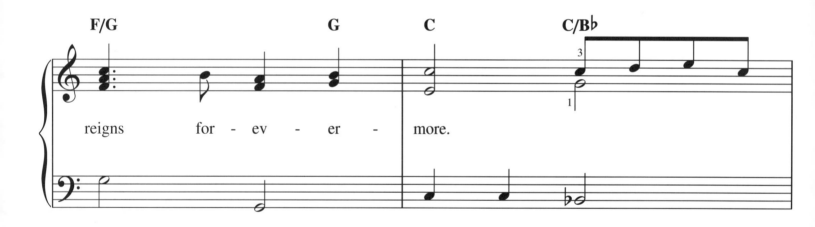

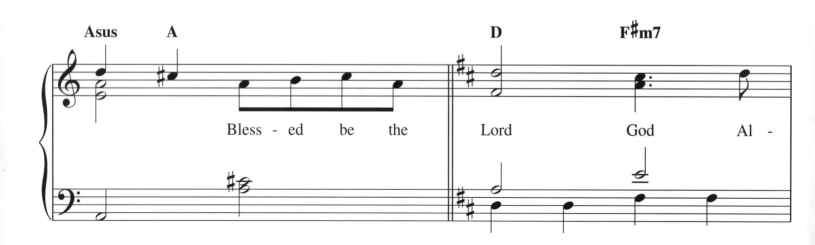

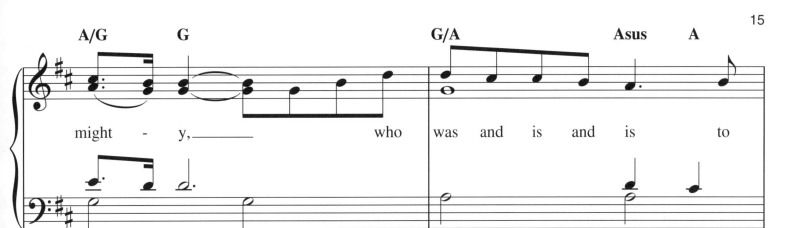

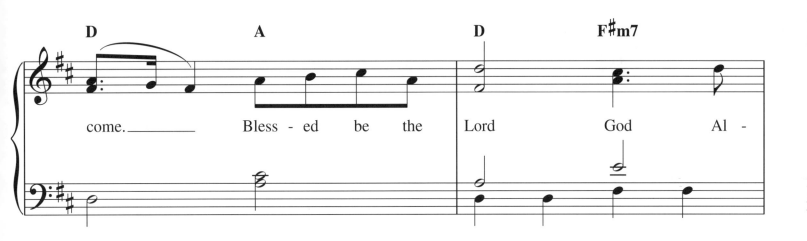

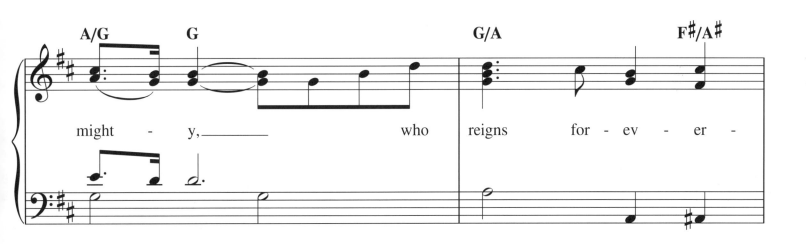

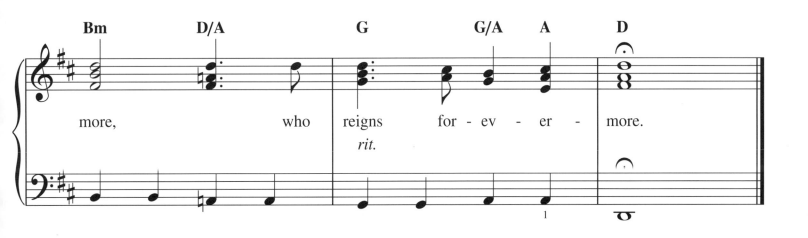

# BLESSED BE THE NAME
# OF THE LORD

Words and Music by
DON MOEN

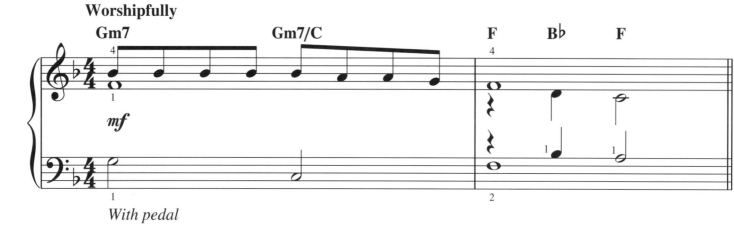

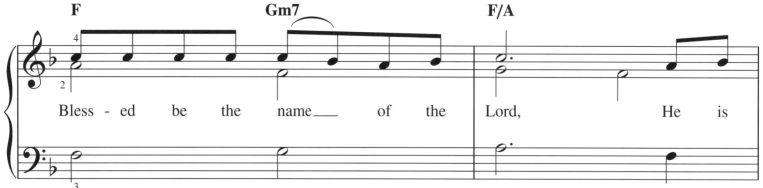

Bless - ed be the name of the Lord, He is

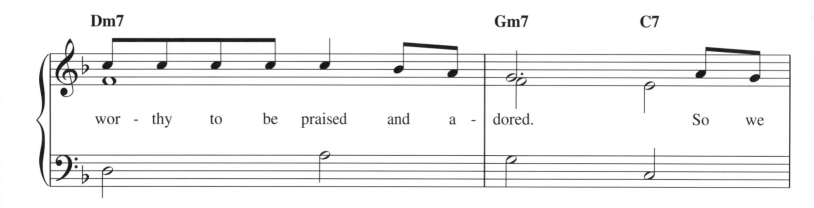

wor - thy to be praised and a - dored. So we

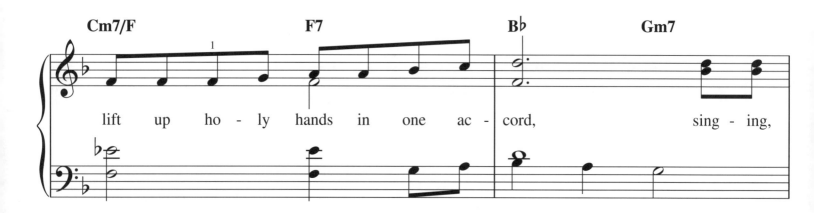

lift up ho - ly hands in one ac - cord, sing - ing,

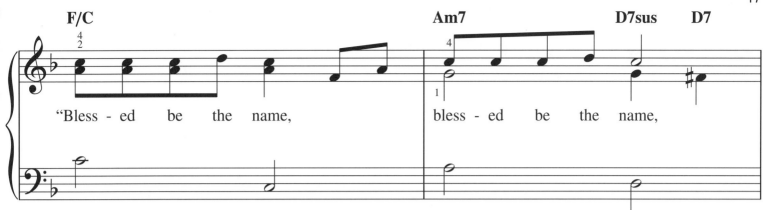

"Bless - ed be the name, bless - ed be the name,

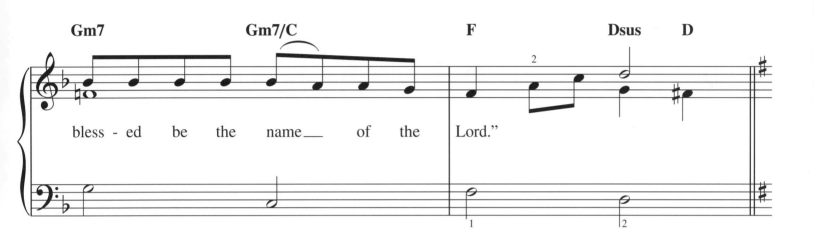

bless - ed be the name____ of the Lord."

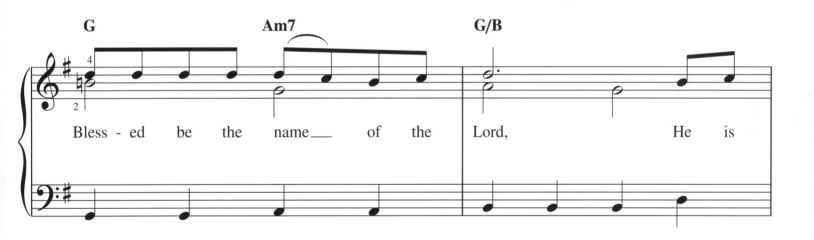

Bless - ed be the name____ of the Lord, He is

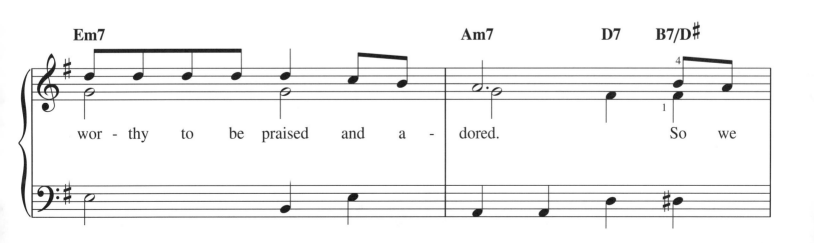

wor - thy to be praised and a - dored. So we

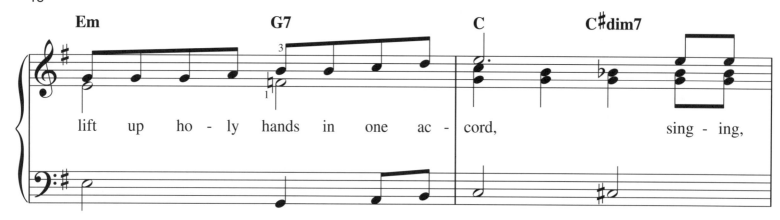

lift up ho - ly hands in one ac - cord, sing - ing,

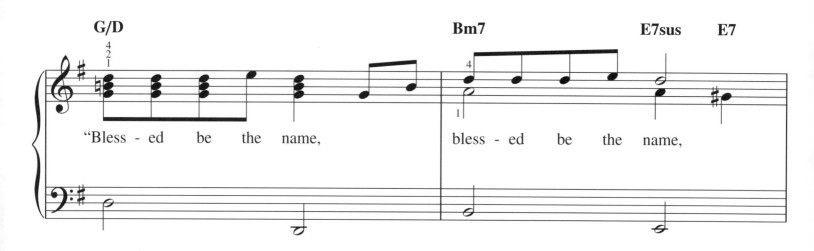

"Bless - ed be the name, bless - ed be the name,

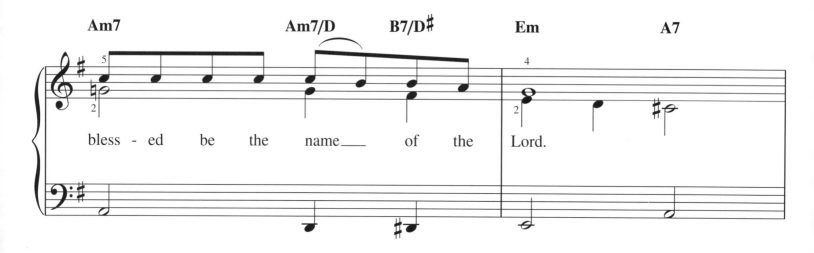

bless - ed be the name___ of the Lord.

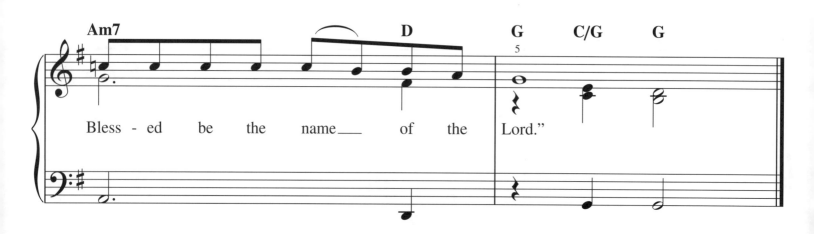

Bless - ed be the name___ of the Lord."

# CELEBRATE JESUS

Words and Music by
GARY OLIVER

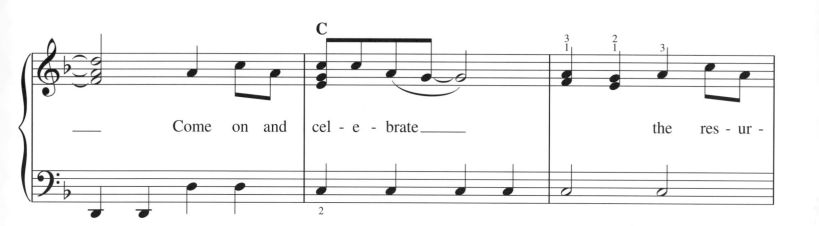

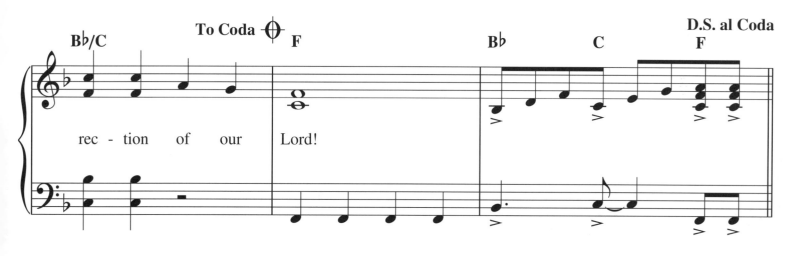

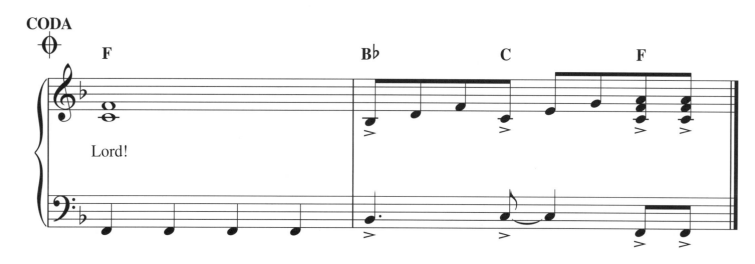

# COME INTO HIS PRESENCE

Words and Music by
LYNN BAIRD

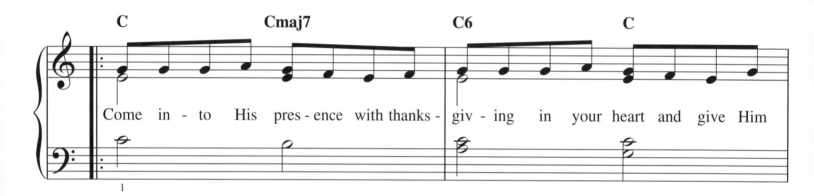

Come in-to His pres-ence with thanks-giv-ing in your heart and give Him

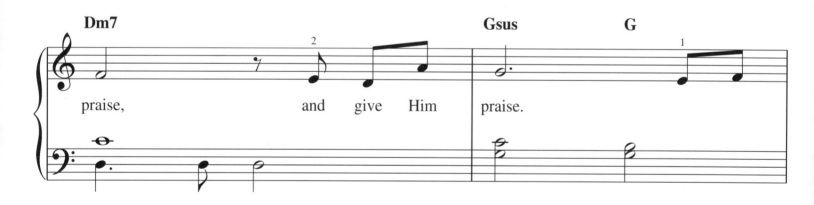

praise, and give Him praise.

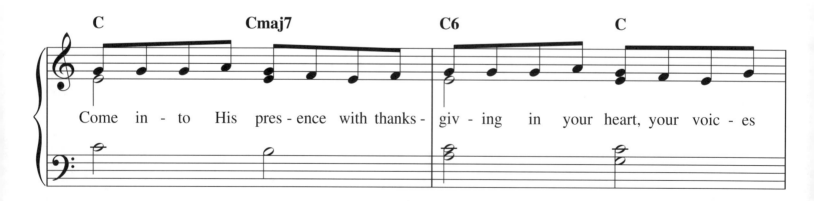

Come in-to His pres-ence with thanks-giv-ing in your heart, your voic-es

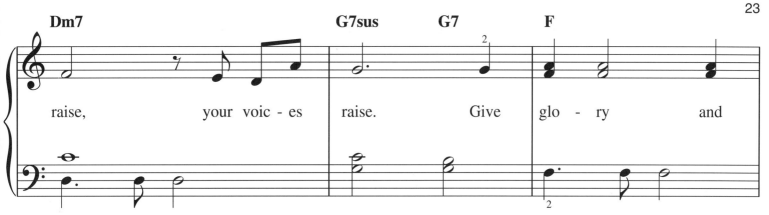

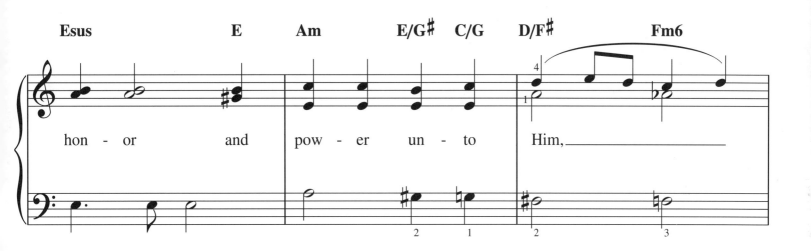

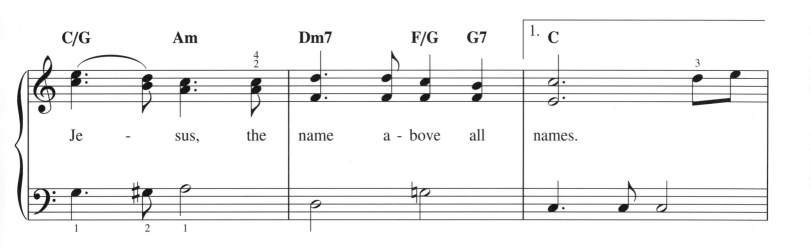

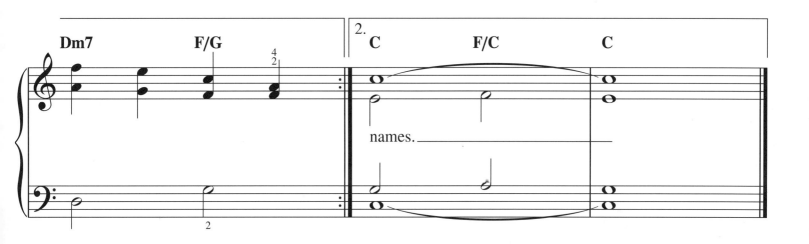

# GOD WILL MAKE A WAY

Words and Music by
DON MOEN

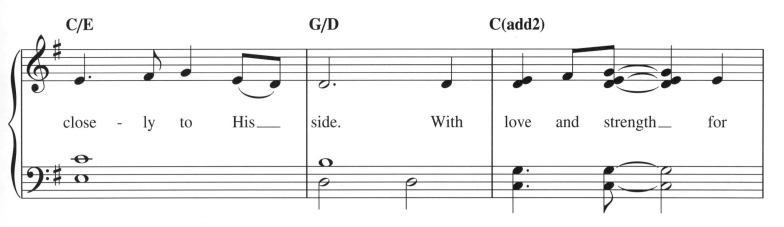

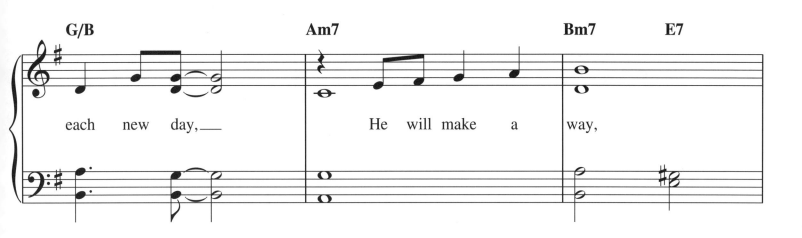

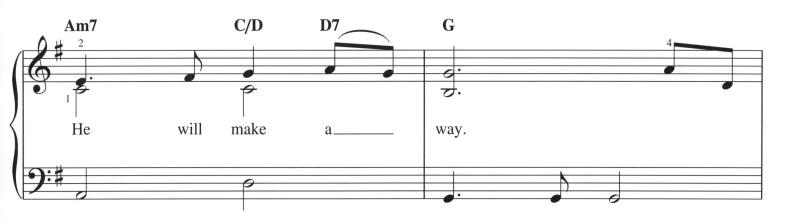

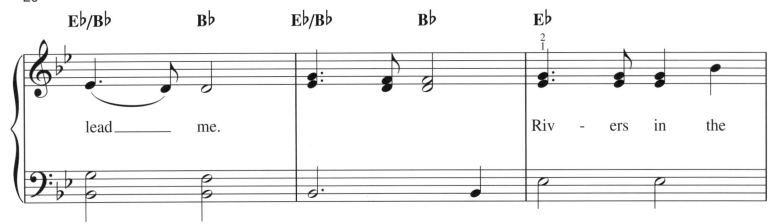

lead_____ me.                    Riv - ers in the

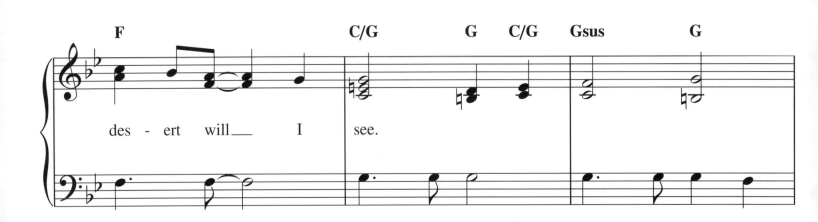

des - ert will__ I    see.

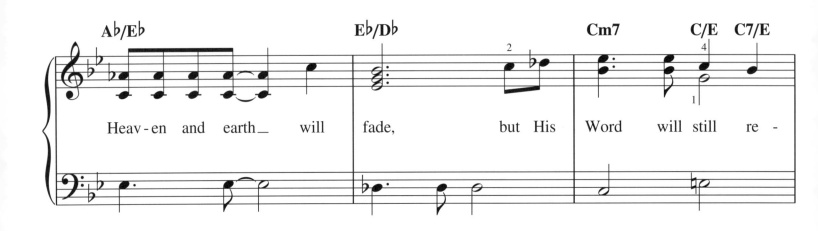

Heav - en and earth__ will    fade,              but His    Word    will still re -

main.                    He  will  do____          some - thing new____    to -

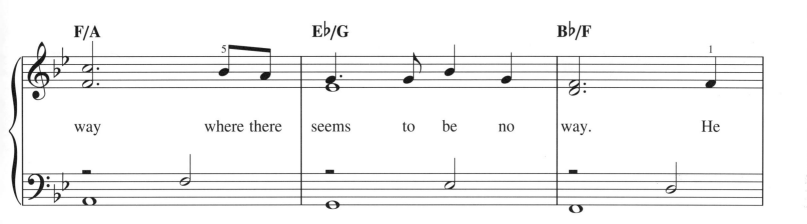

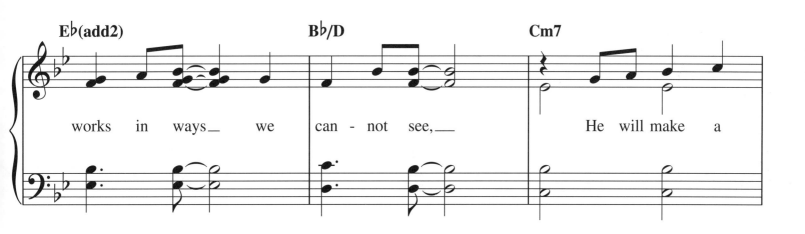

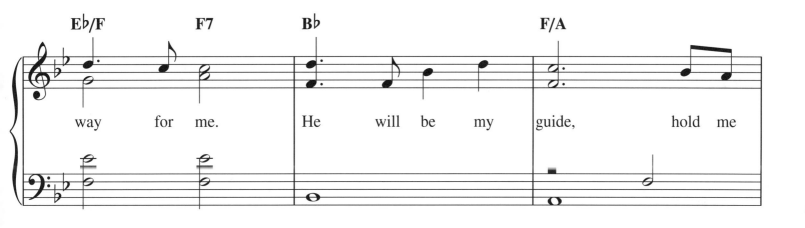

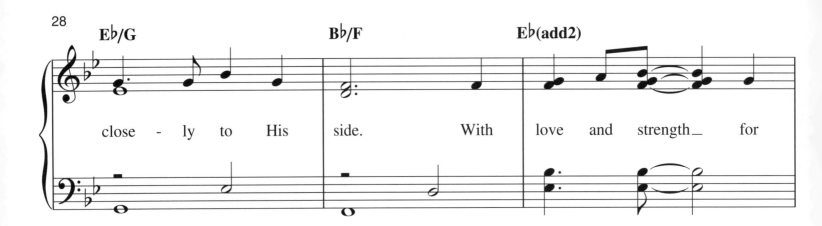

close - ly to His side. With love and strength___ for

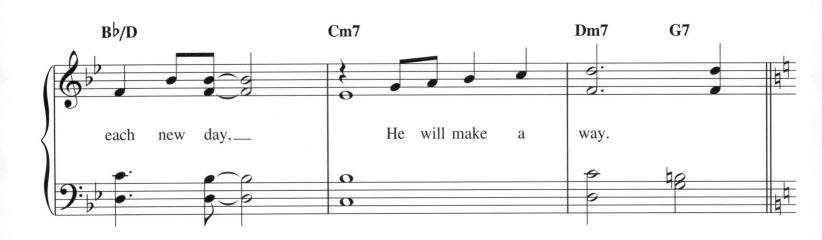

each new day,___ He will make a way.

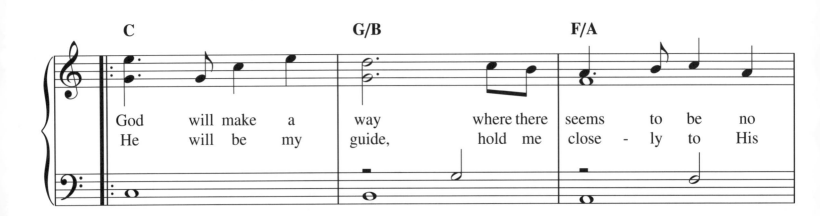

God will make a way where there seems to be no
He will be my guide, hold me close - ly to His

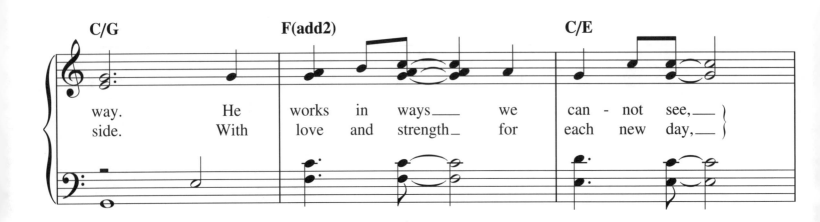

way. He works in ways___ we can - not see,___
side. With love and strength___ for each new day,___

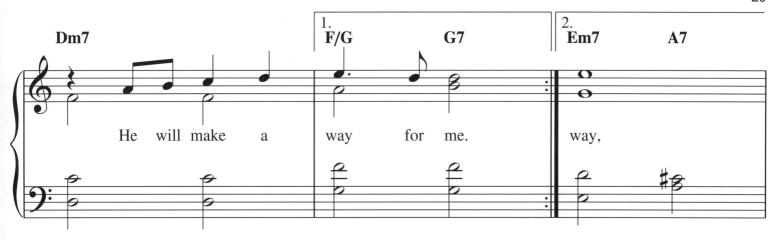

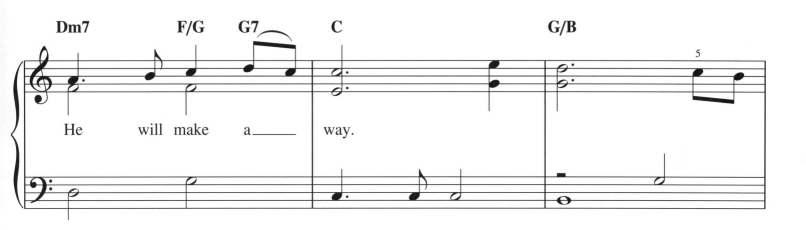

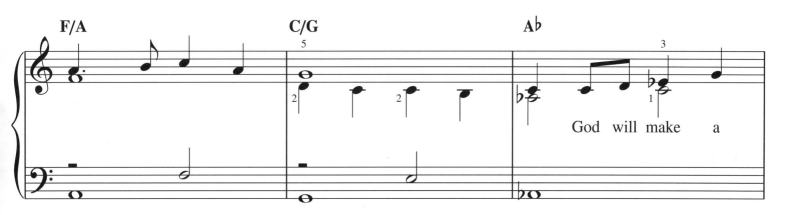

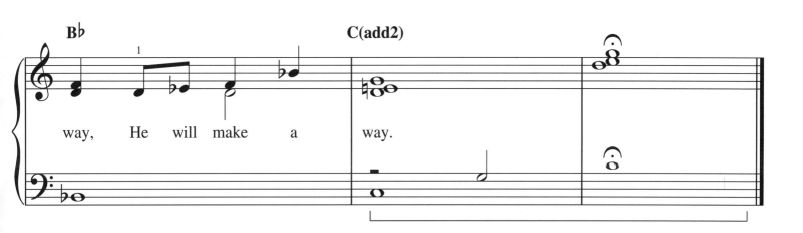

# HOLY SPIRIT RAIN DOWN

Words and Music by
RUSSELL FRAGAR

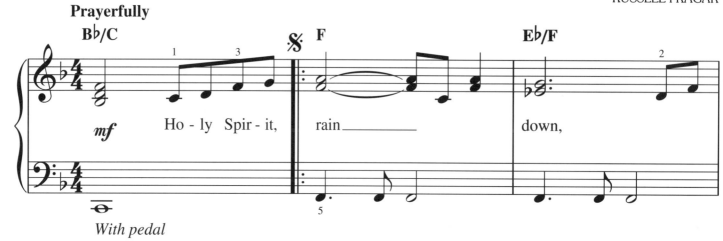

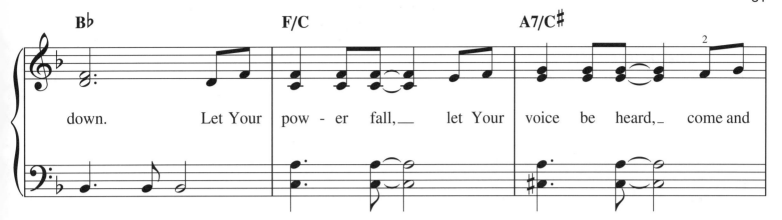

**Bb**  **F/C**  **A7/C#**

down. Let Your pow - er fall,__ let Your voice be heard,__ come and

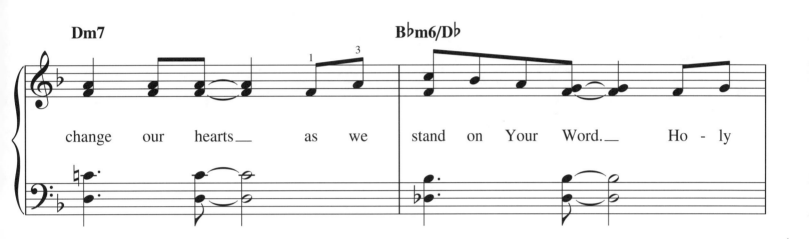

**Dm7**  **Bbm6/Db**

change our hearts__ as we stand on Your Word.__ Ho - ly

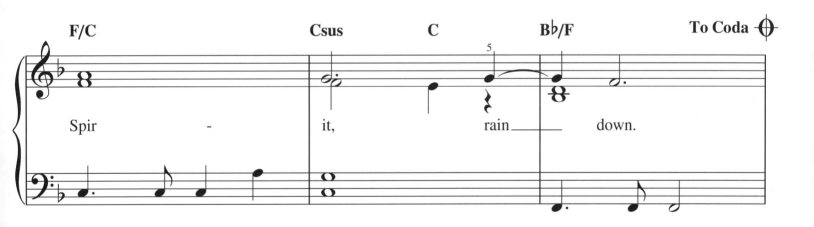

**F/C**  **Csus**  **C**  **Bb/F**  **To Coda ⊕**

Spir - it, rain__ down.

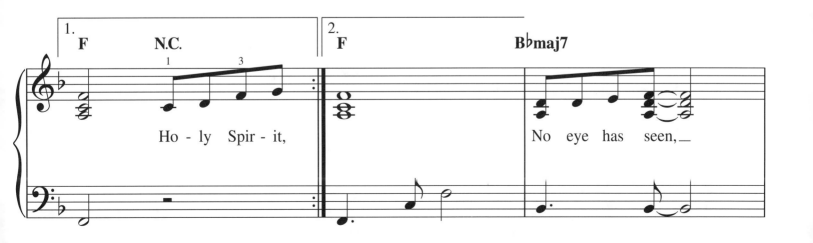

**1. F**  **N.C.**  **2. F**  **Bbmaj7**

Ho - ly Spir - it, No eye has seen,__

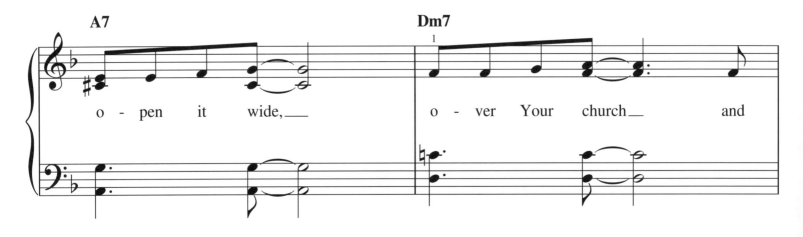

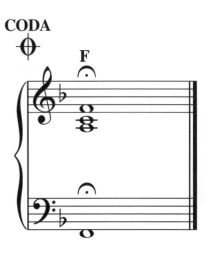

# GIVE THANKS

Words and Music by
HENRY SMITH

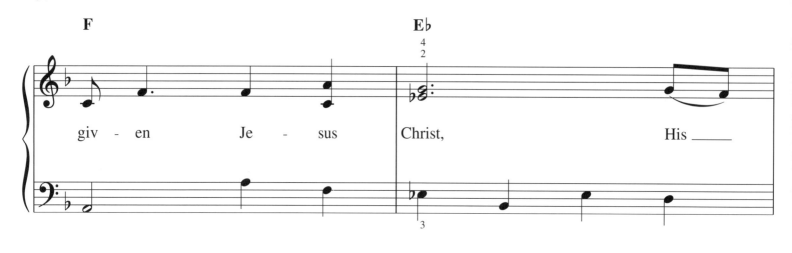

**F**

**E♭**

giv - en    Je - sus    Christ,    His ____

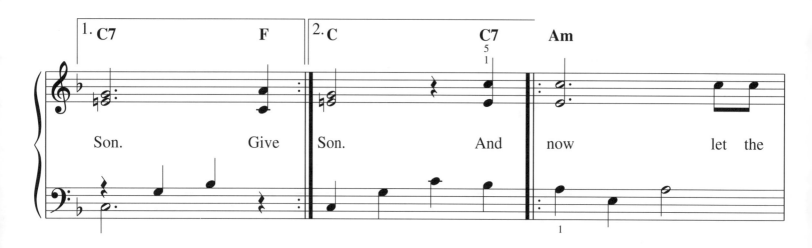

**1. C7**    **F**    **2. C**    **C7**    **Am**

Son.    Give    Son.    And    now    let the

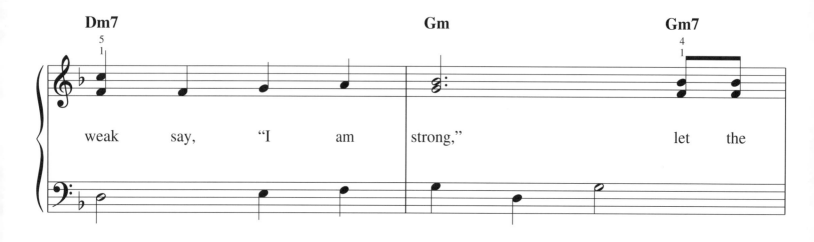

**Dm7**    **Gm**    **Gm7**

weak    say,    "I    am    strong,"    let    the

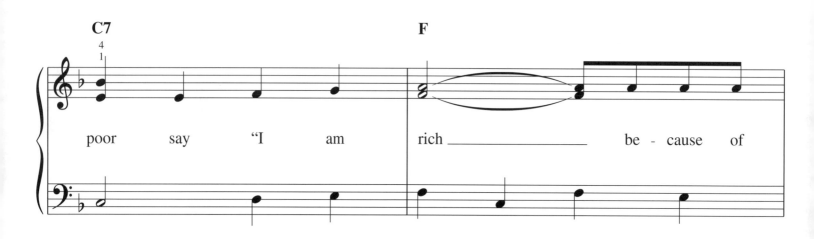

**C7**    **F**

poor    say    "I    am    rich _____    be - cause of

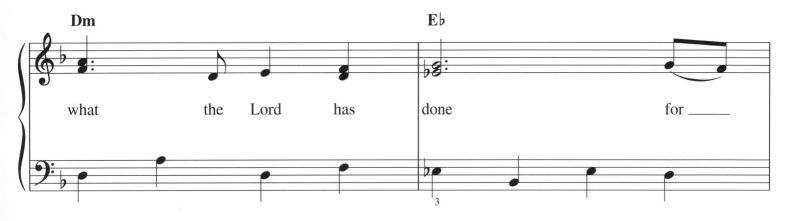

**Dm** ... **Eb**

what the Lord has done for ____

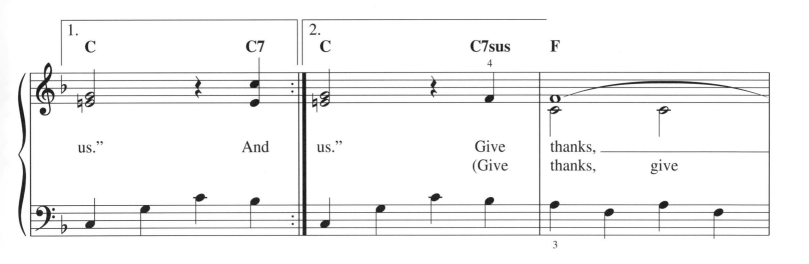

1. **C** ... **C7**
2. **C** ... **C7sus** **F**

us." And us." Give thanks, ____
(Give thanks, give

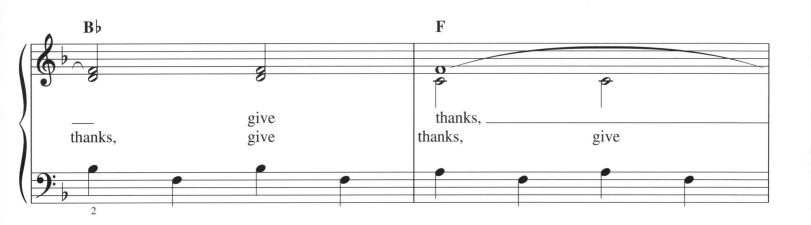

**Bb** ... **F**

____ give thanks, ____
thanks, give thanks, give

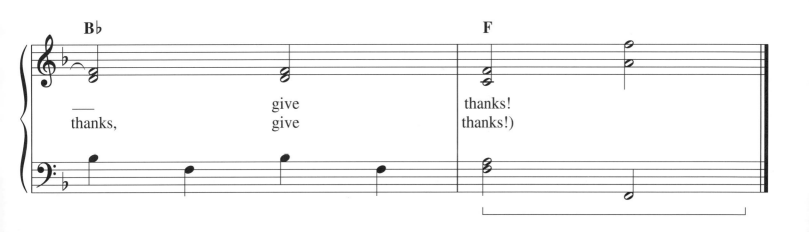

**Bb** ... **F**

____ give thanks!
thanks, give thanks!)

# I SING PRAISES

Words and Music by
TERRY MacALMON

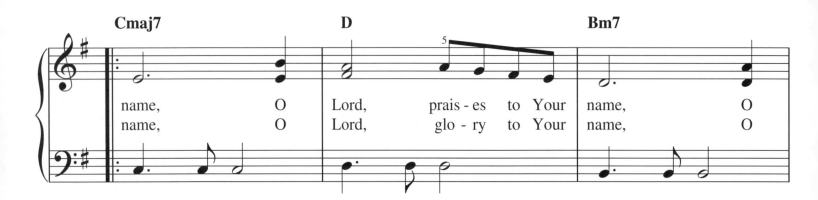

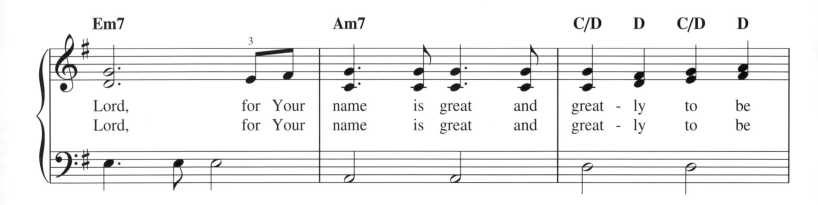

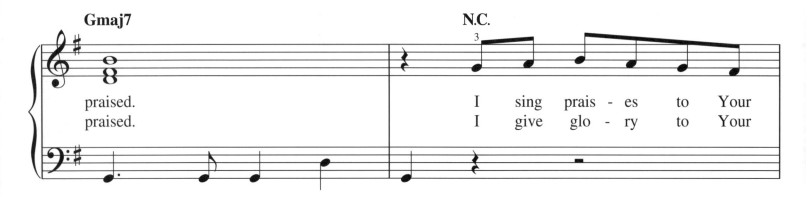

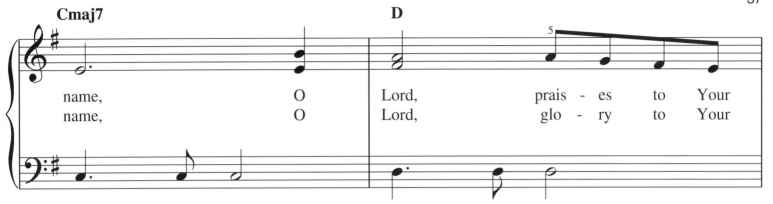

name,      O    Lord,      prais - es    to    Your
name,      O    Lord,      glo - ry    to    Your

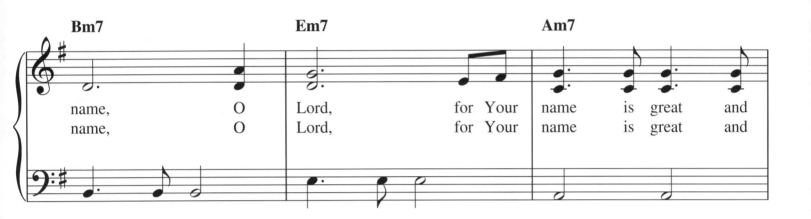

name,      O    Lord,      for Your    name    is   great    and
name,      O    Lord,      for Your    name    is   great    and

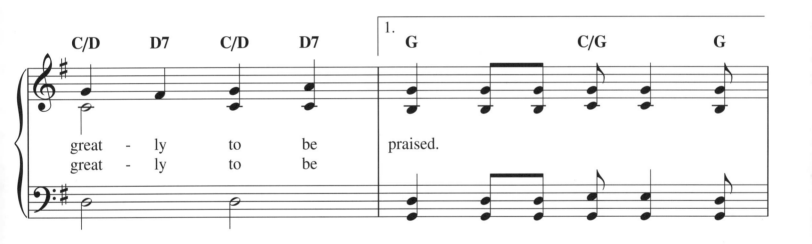

great - ly    to    be     praised.
great - ly    to    be

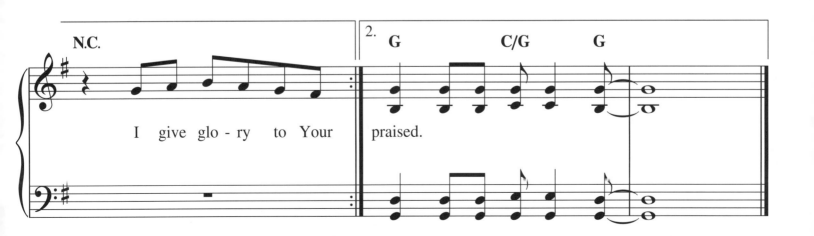

I   give glo - ry    to Your     praised.

# I WORSHIP YOU, ALMIGHTY GOD

Words and Music by
SONDRA CORBETT-WOOD

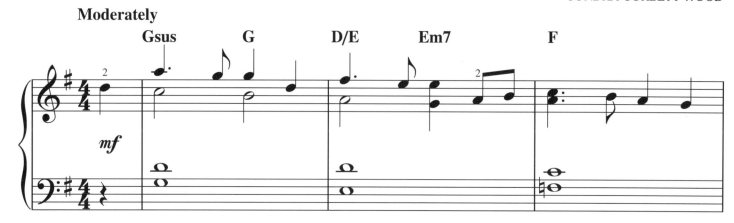

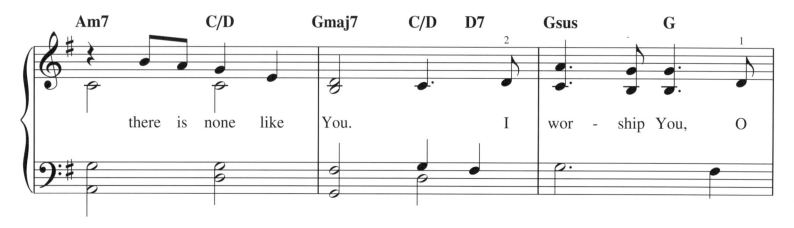

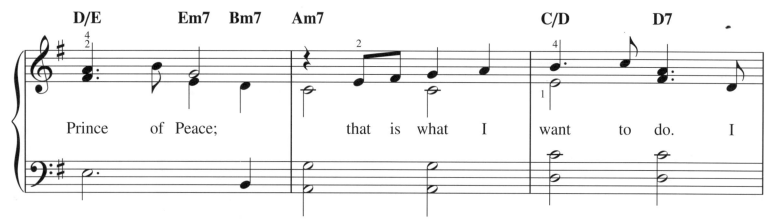

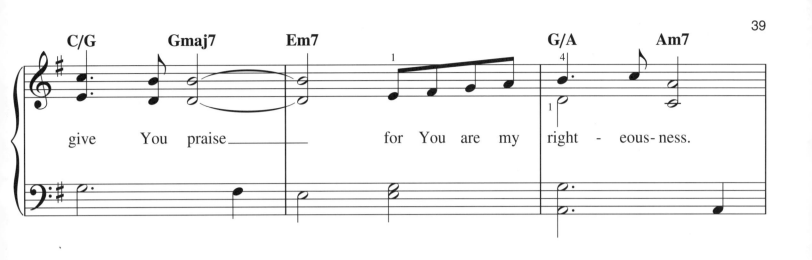

give You praise_____ for You are my right - eous-ness.

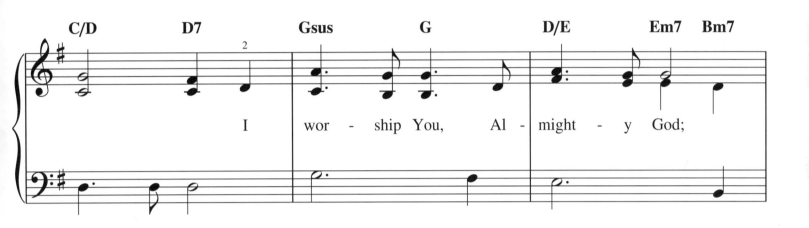

I wor - ship You, Al - might - y God;

there is none like You. I

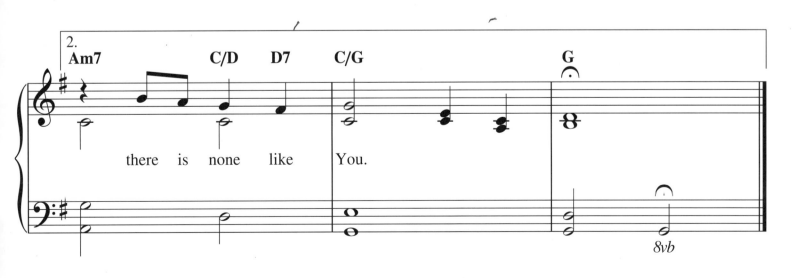

there is none like You.

*8vb*

# JESUS IS ALIVE

Words and Music by
RON KENOLY

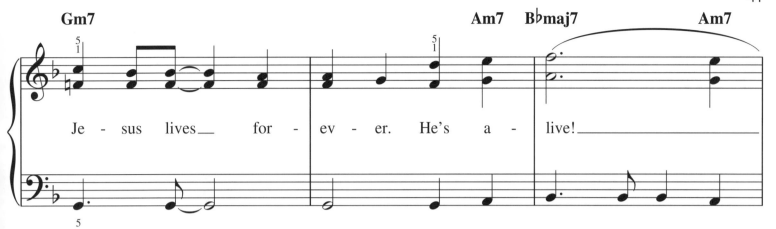

Je - sus lives__ for - ev - er. He's a - live!__

__ He's a - live!__ He's the

Al - pha and O - me - ga,__ the First and Last__ is

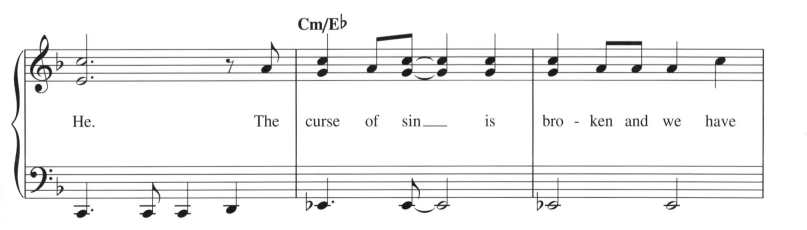

He. The curse of sin__ is bro - ken and we have

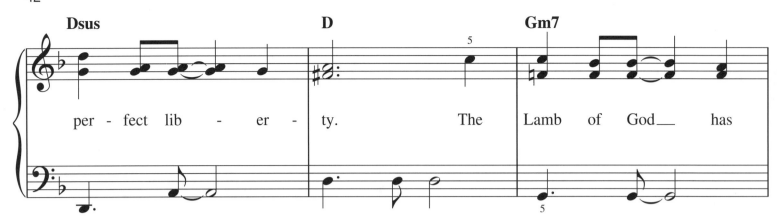

per - fect lib - er - ty. The Lamb of God__ has

ris - en. He's a - live!__ He's a -

live!__ Hal - le - live!__ Hal - le -

lu - jah! Je - sus is a - live!

# JESUS, NAME ABOVE ALL NAMES

Words and Music by
NAIDA HEARN

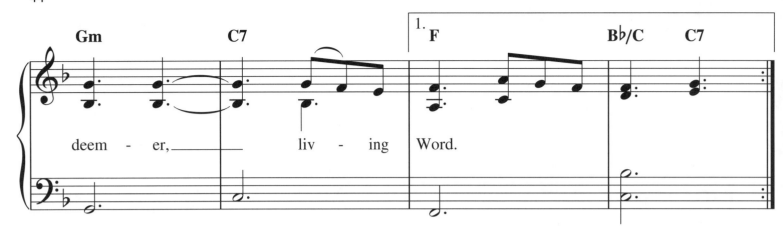

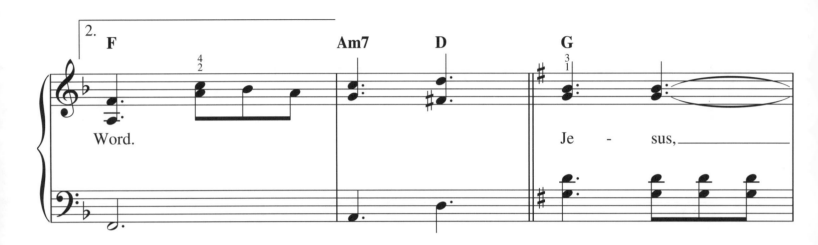

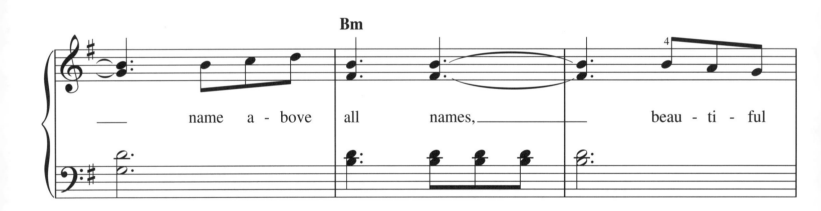

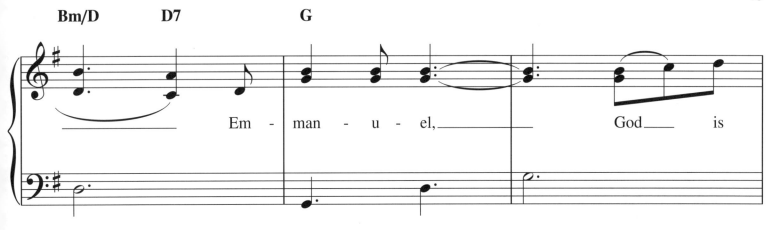

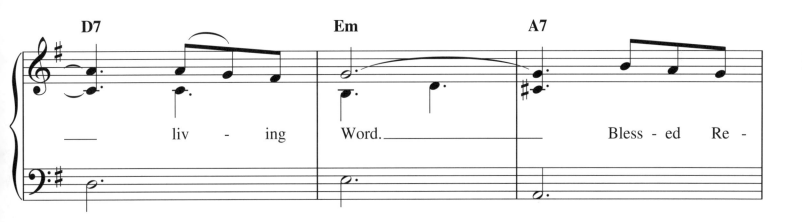

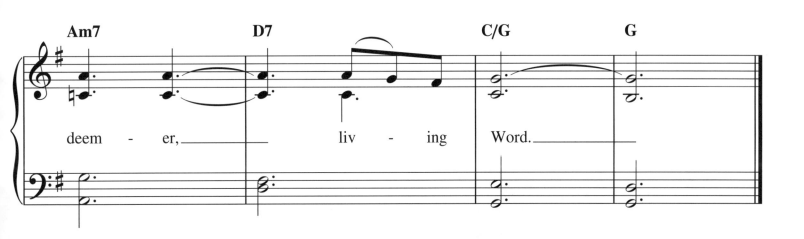

# LET THERE BE GLORY AND HONOR AND PRAISES

Words and Music by
ELIZABETH GREENELSH

© 1978 Integrity's Hosanna! Music/ASCAP
c/o Integrity Media, Inc., 1000 Cody Road, Mobile, AL 36695

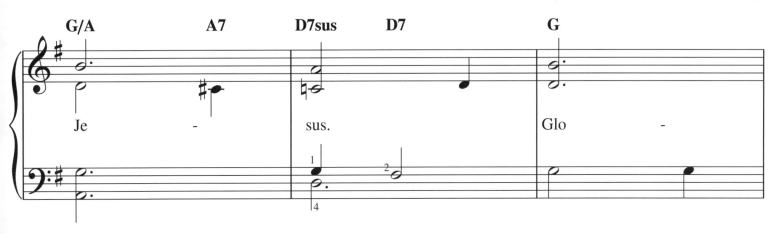

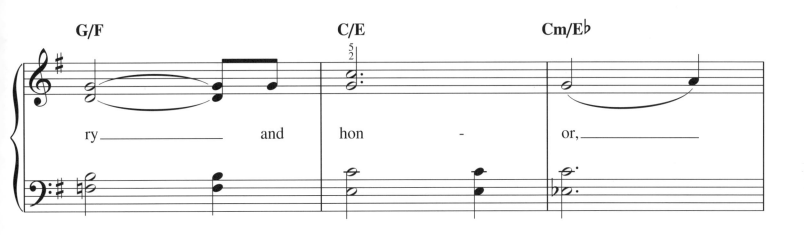

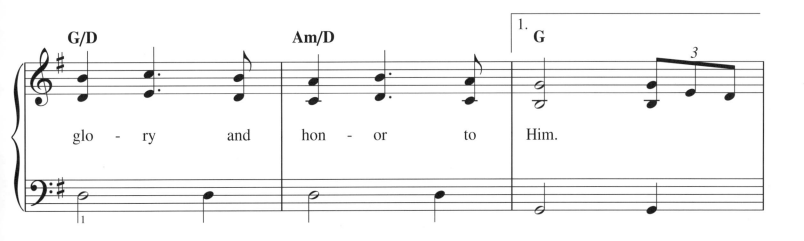

# THE LORD REIGNS

Words and Music by
DAN STRADWICK

**To Coda**

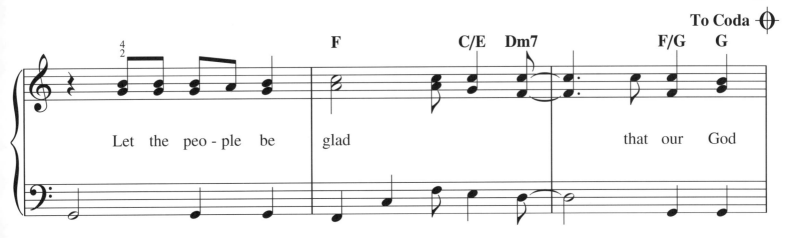

Let the peo - ple be glad that our God

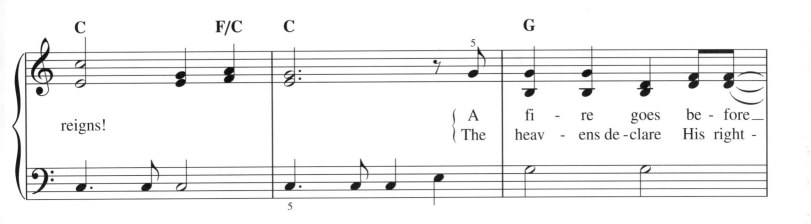

reigns!

A fi - re goes be - fore
The heav - ens de - clare His right -

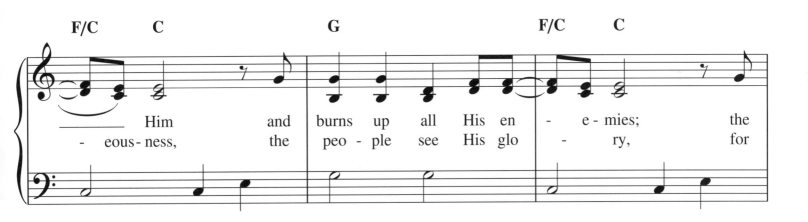

_____ Him and burns up all His en - e - mies; the
- eous - ness, and the peo - ple see His glo - ry, for

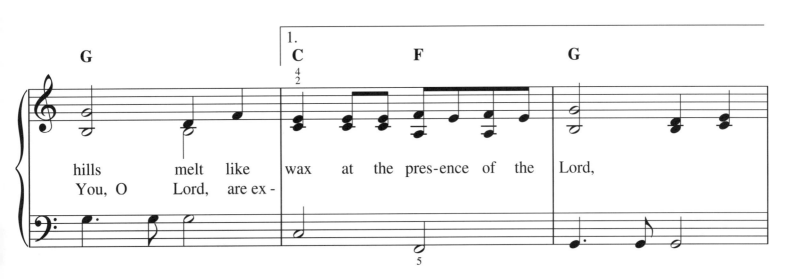

hills melt like wax at the pres - ence of the Lord,
You, O Lord, are ex -

at the pres-ence of the Lord!                                        The

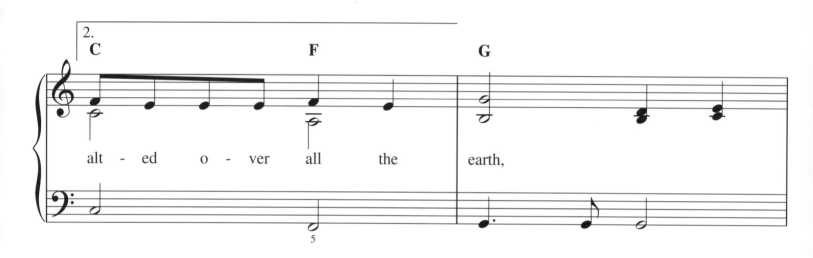

**2.**
C                          F            G

alt - ed    o - ver   all    the    earth,

**D.S. al Coda**

o - ver   all    the    earth!                                      The

**CODA**
C                    F/G          G      C      Gm7        C

reigns!                          Our God  reigns!

# MORE PRECIOUS THAN SILVER

Words and Music by
LYNN DeSHAZO

**Warmly, with expression**

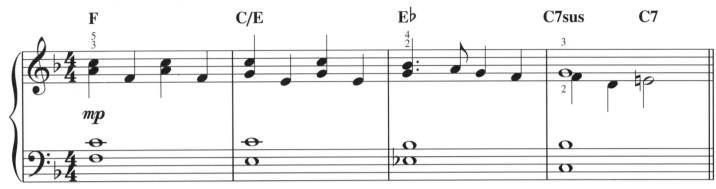

With pedal

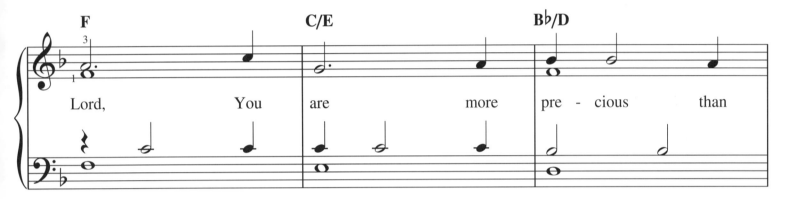

Lord, You are more pre - cious than

sil - ver. Lord, You are more

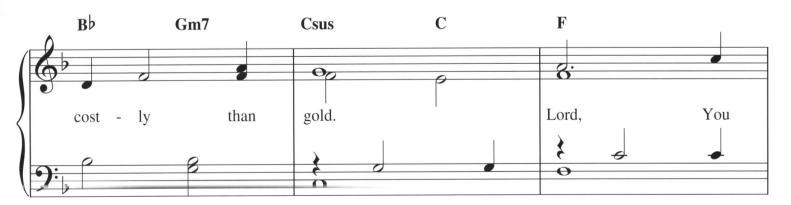

cost - ly than gold. Lord, You

are　　　more　beau - ti - ful＿＿ than　dia - monds, and

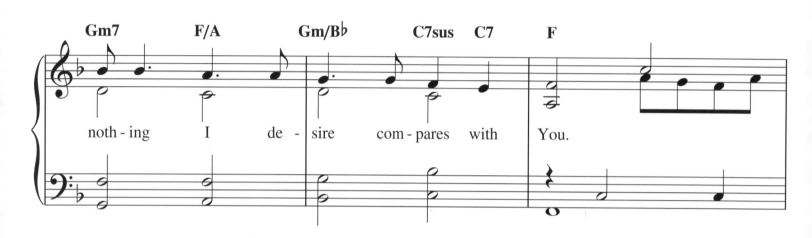

noth - ing　I　de - sire　com - pares　with　You.

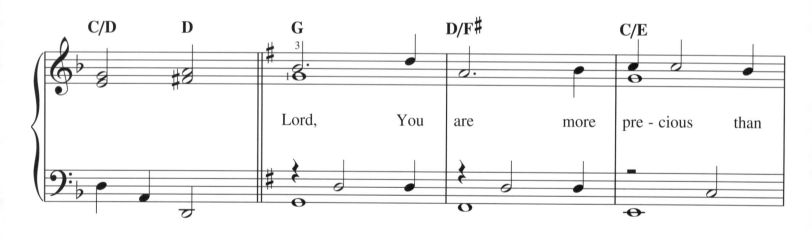

Lord,　　You　are　more　pre - cious　than

sil - ver.　　Lord,　You　are　more

53

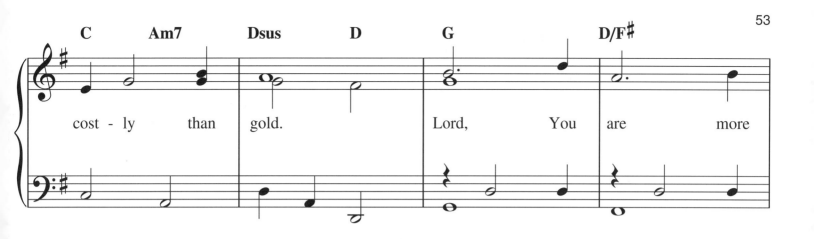

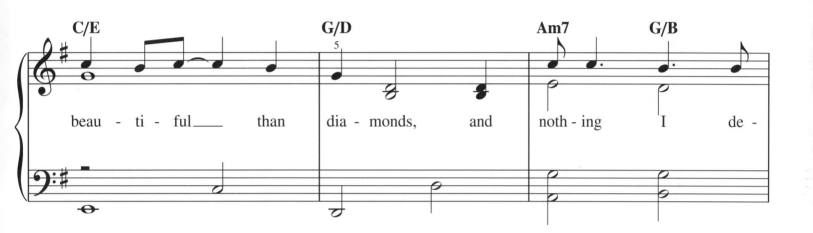

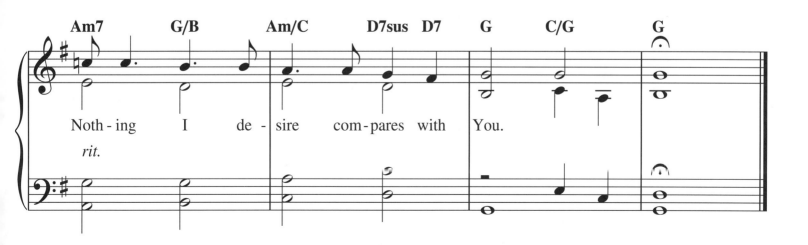

# MY LIFE IS IN YOU, LORD

Words and Music by
DANIEL GARDNER

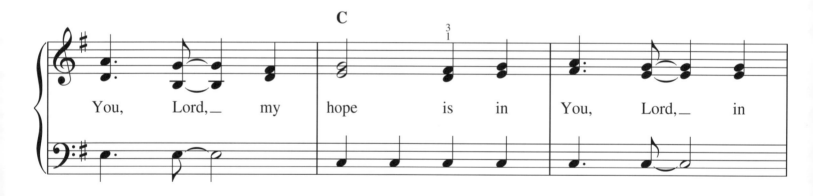

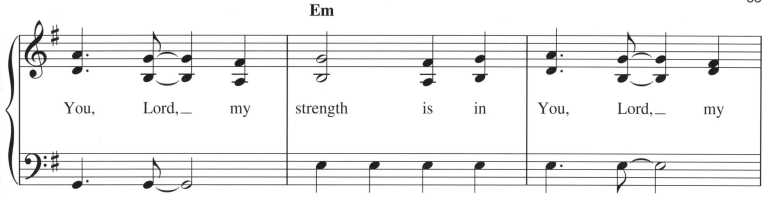

You, Lord, __ my strength is in You, Lord, __ my

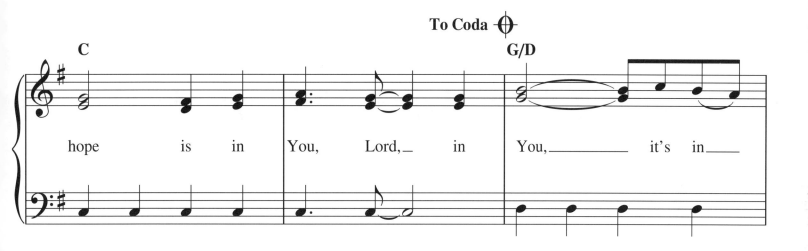

hope is in You, Lord, __ in You, _____ it's in ____

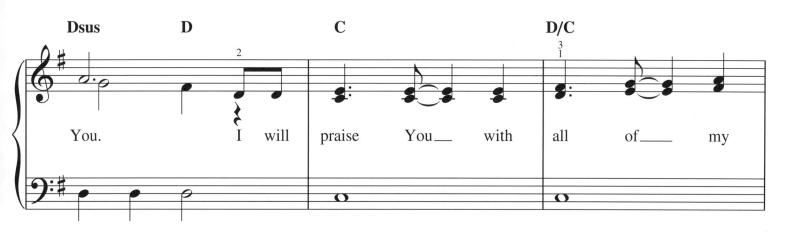

You. I will praise You __ with all of ____ my

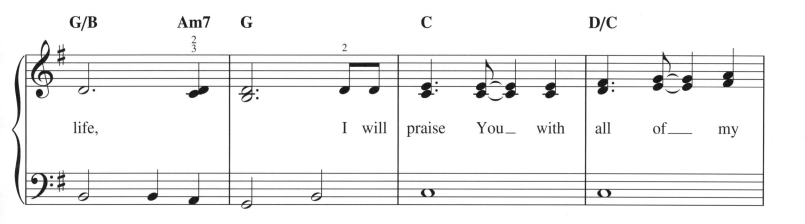

life, I will praise You __ with all of ____ my

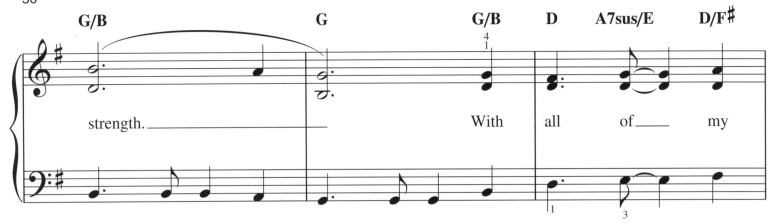

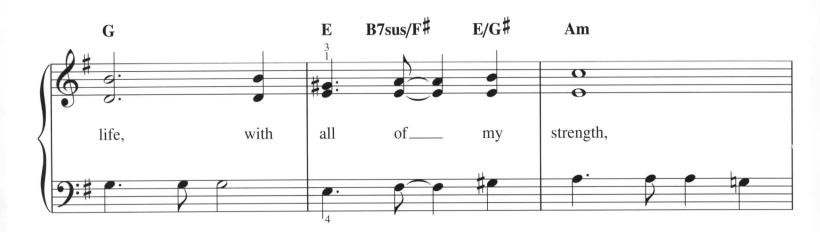

# MY REDEEMER LIVES

Words and Music by
REUBEN MORGAN

I know He res - cued my soul.

His blood has cov - ered my sin. I be -

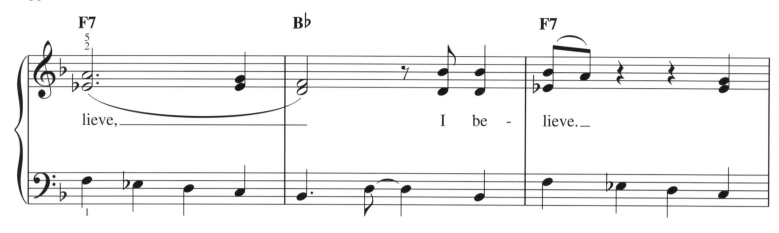

lieve,_____ I be - lieve._

My shame He's tak - en a - way._

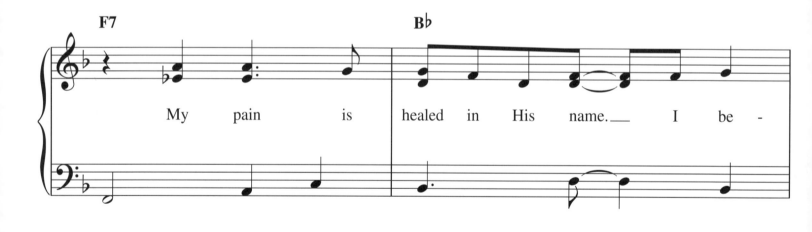

My pain is healed in His name._ I be -

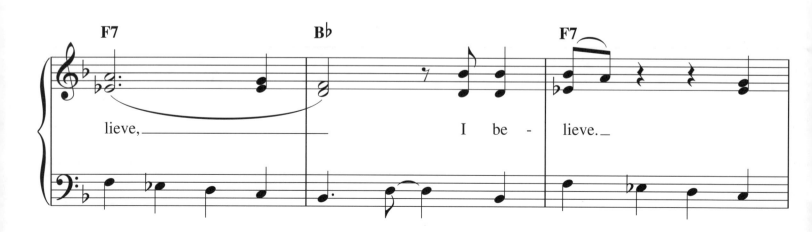

lieve,_____ I be - lieve._

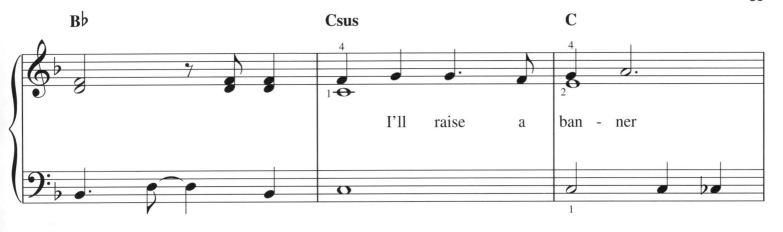

I'll raise a ban - ner

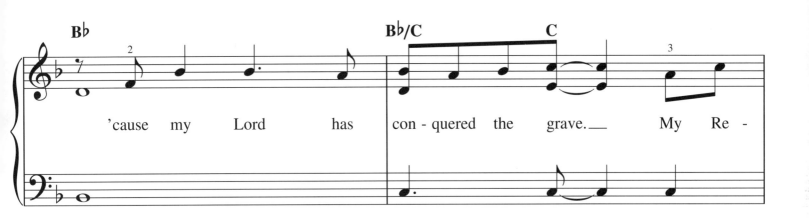

'cause my Lord has con - quered the grave.___ My Re -

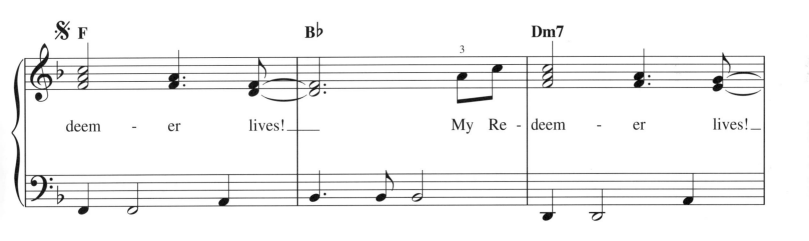

deem - er lives!___ My Re - deem - er lives!___

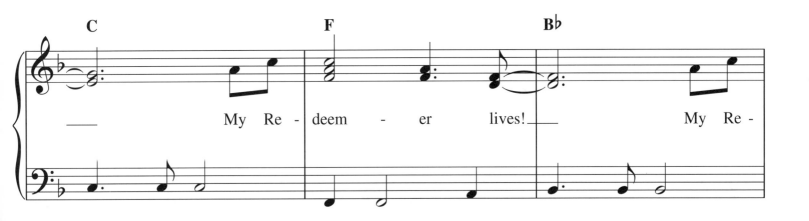

My Re - deem - er lives!___ My Re -

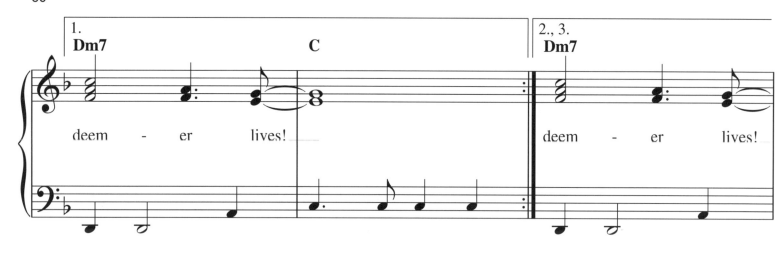

deem - er lives!     deem - er lives!

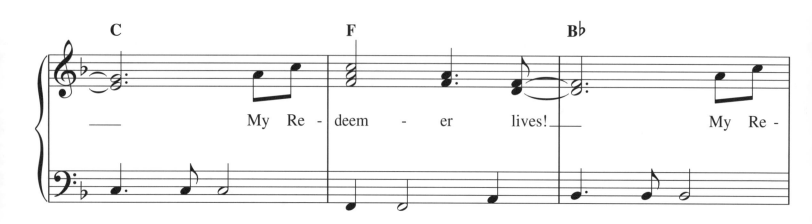

My Re - deem - er lives!     My Re -

deem - er lives!     My Re - deem - er lives!

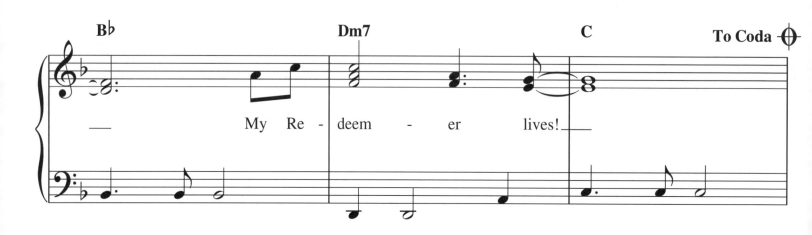

My Re - deem - er lives!

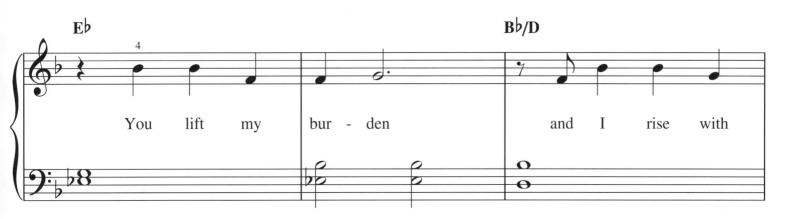

You lift my bur - den and I rise with

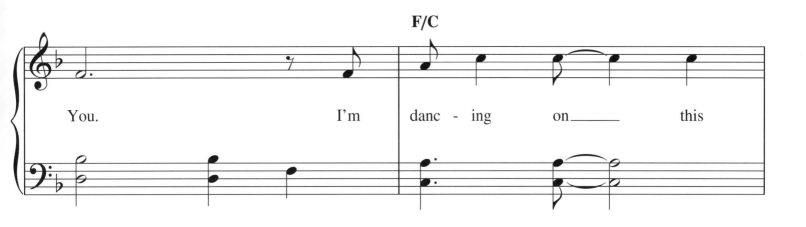

You. I'm danc - ing on_____ this

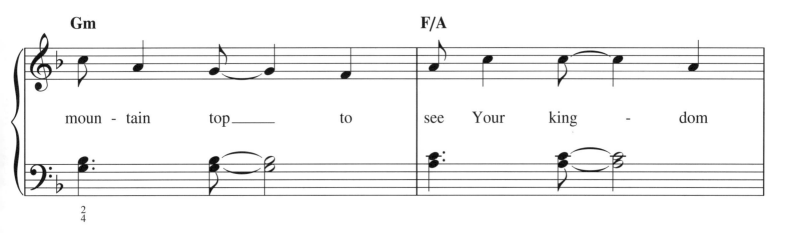

moun - tain top_____ to see Your king - dom

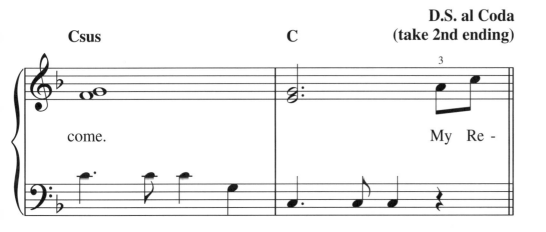

come. My Re -

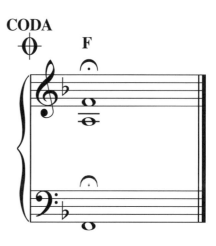

# SHINE, JESUS, SHINE

Words and Music by
GRAHAM KENDRICK

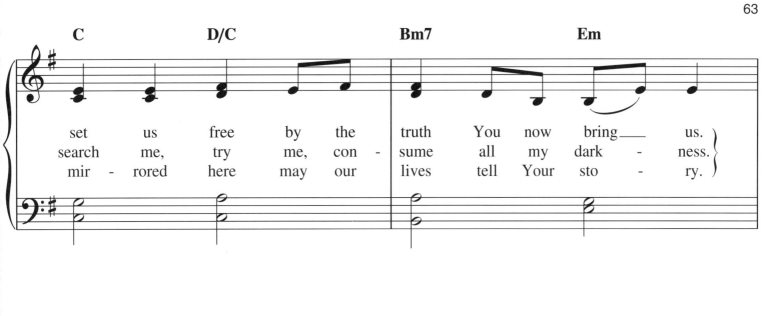

C      D/C      Bm7      Em

set      us      free      by      the      truth      You      now      bring___      us.
search      me,      try      me,      con -      sume      all      my      dark -      ness.
mir - rored      here      may      our      lives      tell      Your      sto -      ry.

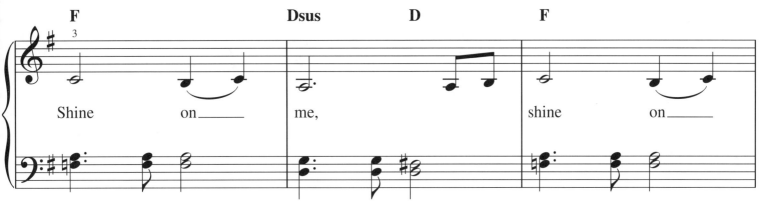

F      Dsus      D      F

Shine      on_____      me,      shine      on_____

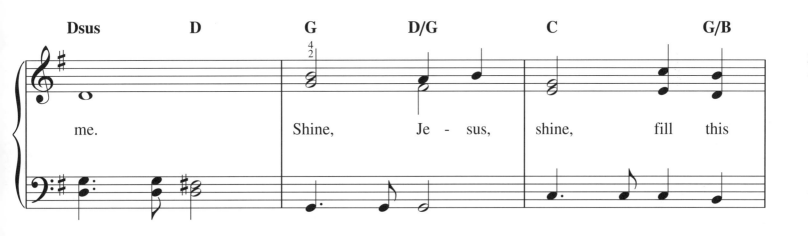

Dsus      D      G      D/G      C      G/B

me.      Shine,      Je - sus,      shine,      fill      this

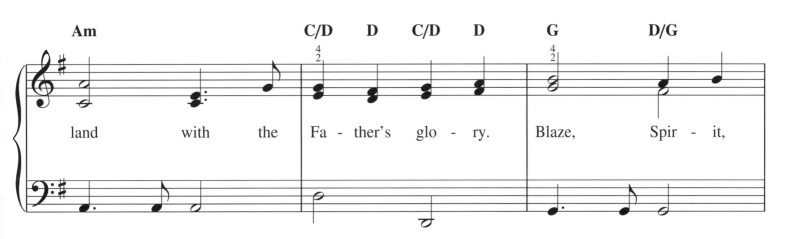

Am      C/D      D      C/D      D      G      D/G

land      with      the      Fa - ther's      glo - ry.      Blaze,      Spir - it,

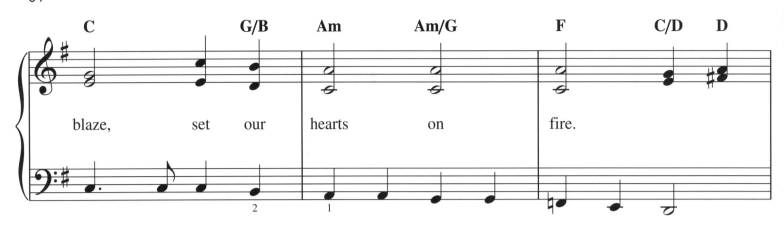

blaze,    set    our    hearts    on    fire.

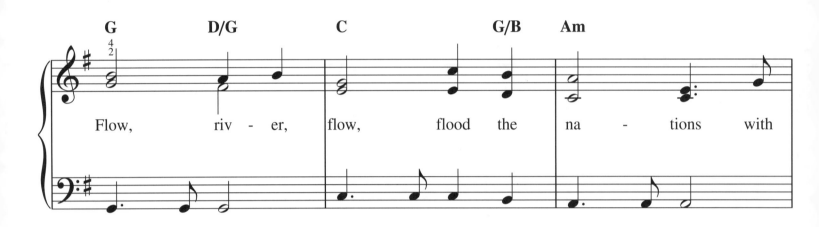

Flow,    riv - er,    flow,    flood the    na - tions    with

grace    and    mer - cy.    Send    forth Your    Word,    Lord, and

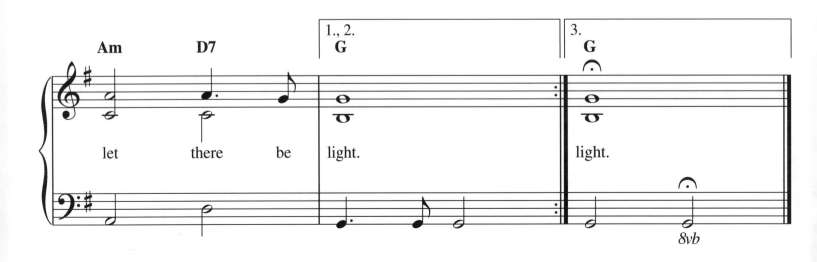

let    there    be    light.    light.

*8vb*

# THIS IS HOW WE OVERCOME

Words and Music by
REUBEN MORGAN

Your light broke through my night, re-
Your hand lift - ed me up; I

stored ex - ceed - ing joy.
stand on high - er ground.

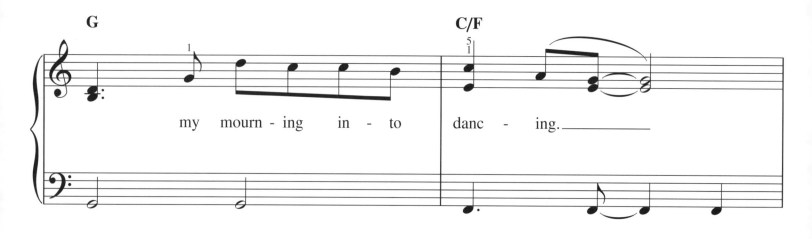

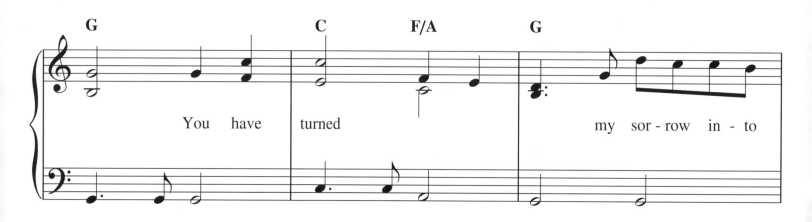

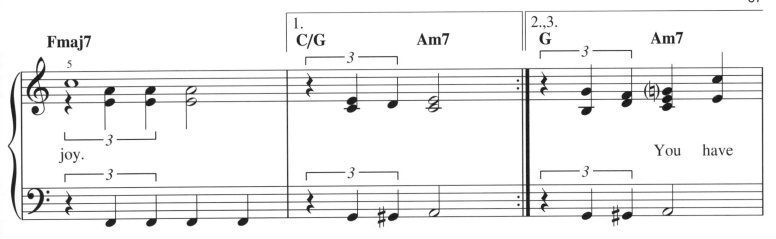

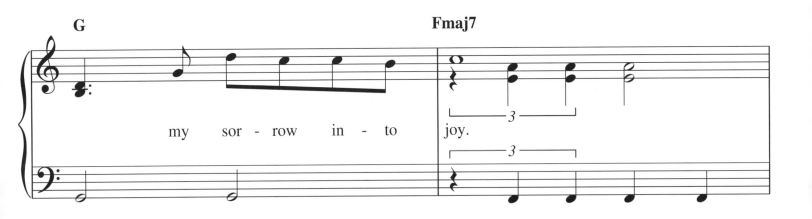

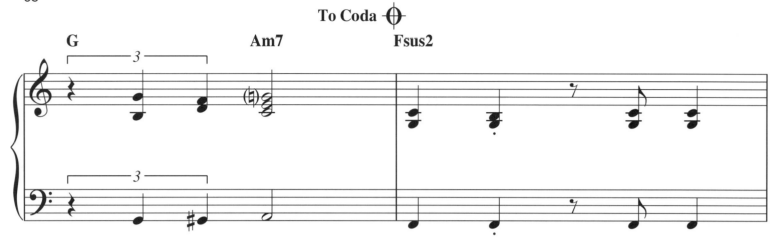

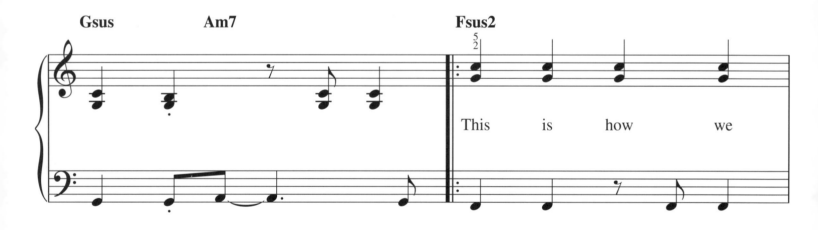

This is how we

o - ver - come.

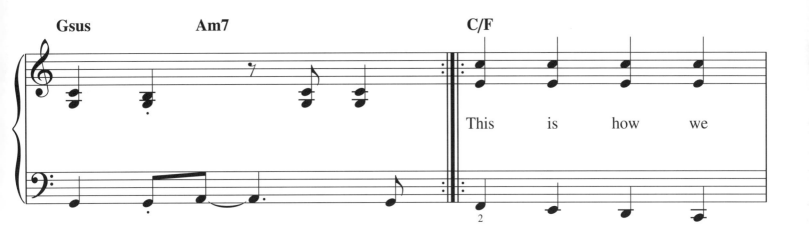

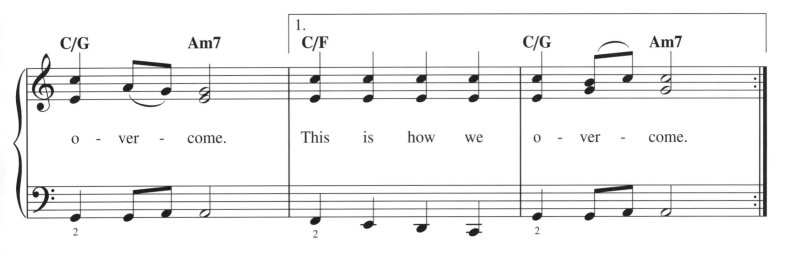

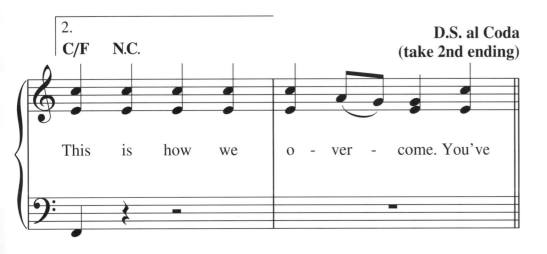

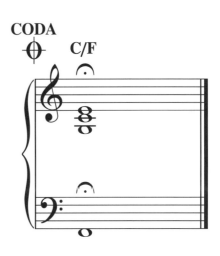

# SHOUT TO THE LORD

Words and Music by
DARLENE ZSCHECH

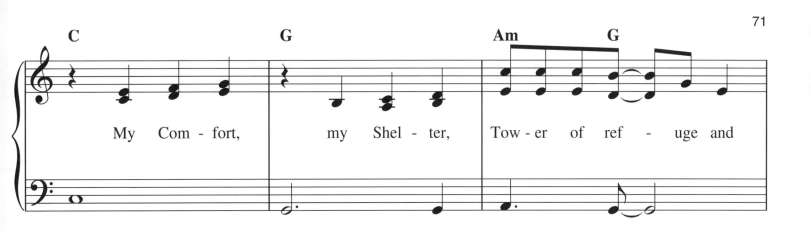

My Com - fort, my Shel - ter, Tow - er of ref - uge and

strength, let ev -'ry breath, all that I am, nev - er cease to

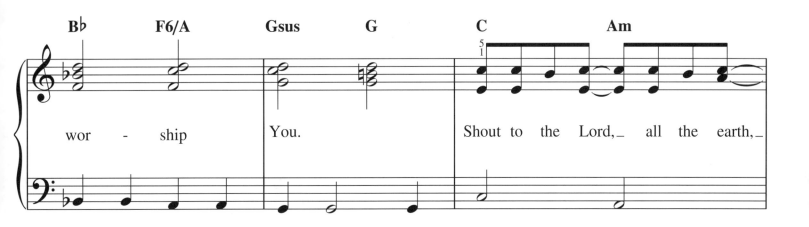

wor - ship You. Shout to the Lord, all the earth,

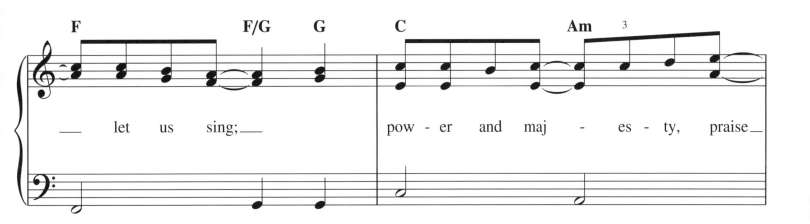

let us sing; pow - er and maj - es - ty, praise

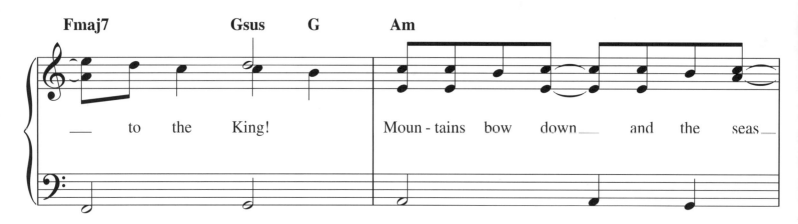

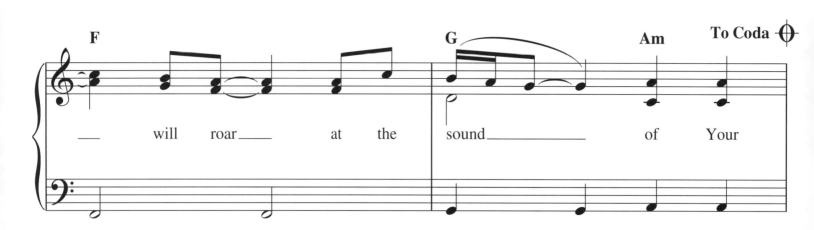

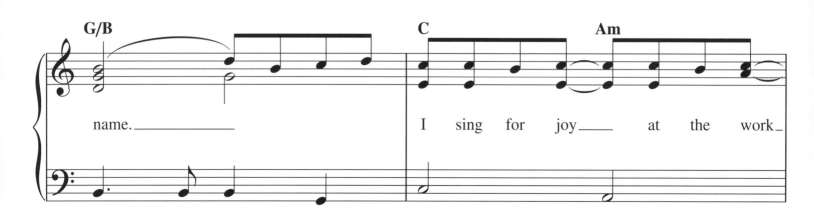

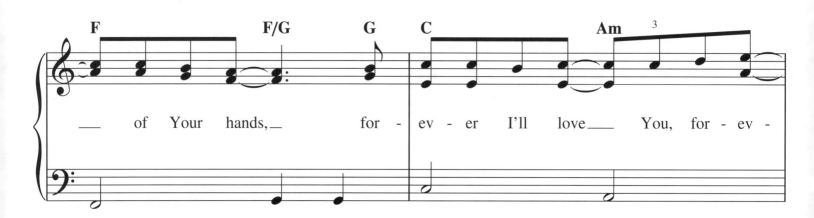

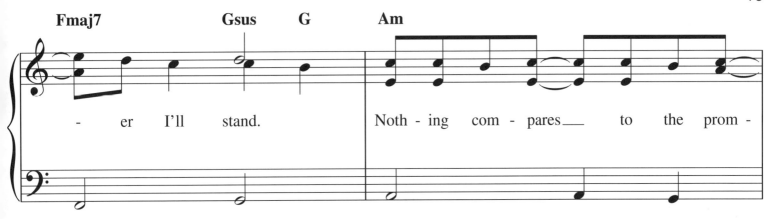

-er I'll stand. Noth - ing com - pares___ to the prom -

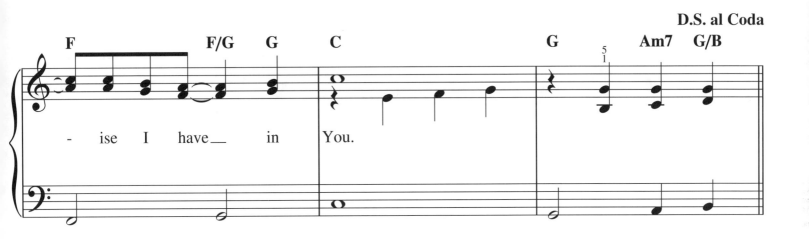

-ise I have___ in You.

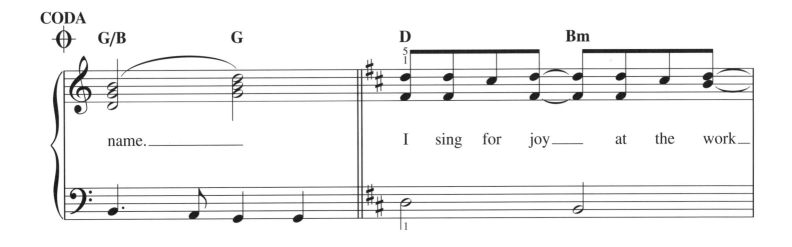

name.___ I sing for joy___ at the work___

___ of Your hands,___ for - ev - er I'll love___ You, for - ev -

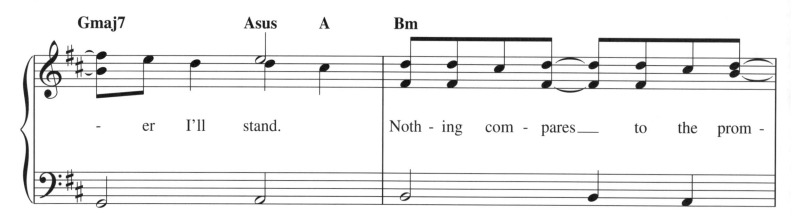

- er I'll stand. Noth - ing com - pares___ to the prom -

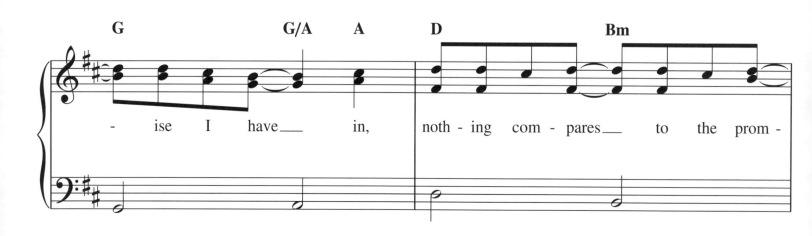

- ise I have___ in, noth - ing com - pares___ to the prom -

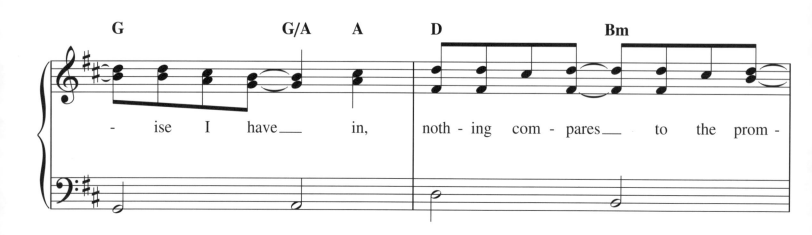

- ise I have___ in, noth - ing com - pares___ to the prom -

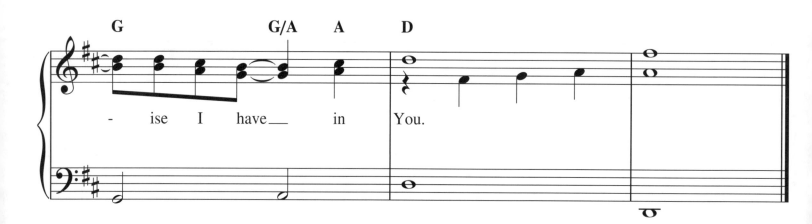

- ise I have___ in You.

# VICTORY CHANT

Words and Music by
JOSEPH VOGELS

**Moderately, in 2**

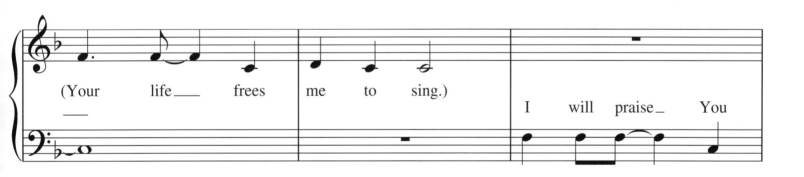

per - fect___ in all Your ways.___ (You're per - fect___ in

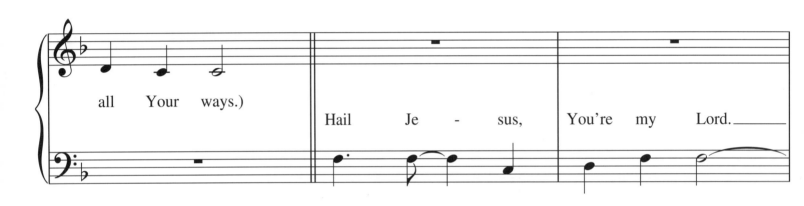

all Your ways.) Hail Je - sus, You're my Lord.___

(Hail Je - sus, You're my Lord.) I will___ o - bey Your Word.___

(I will___ o - bey Your Word.) I want to see___ Your

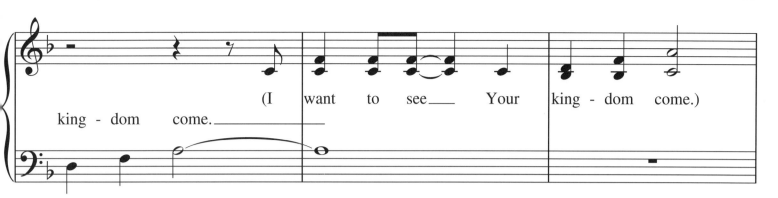

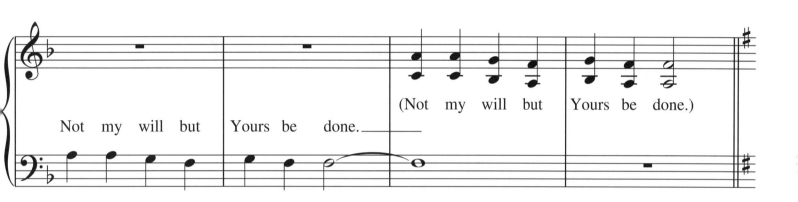

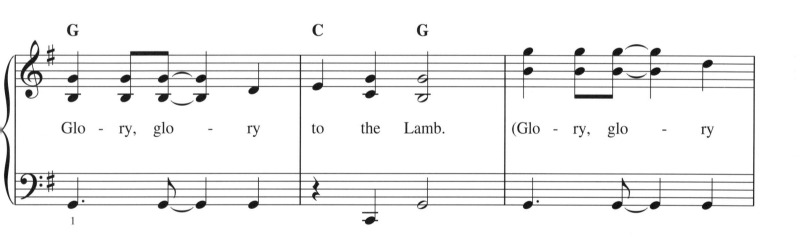

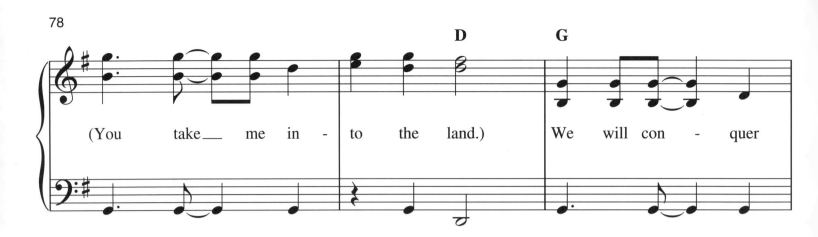

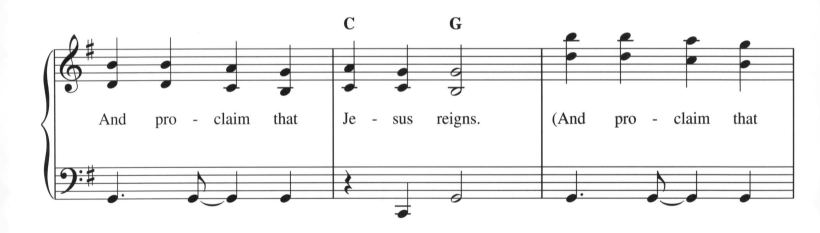

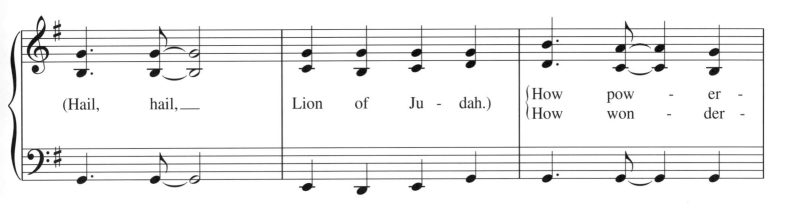

(Hail, hail,___ Lion of Ju - dah.) {How pow - er - / How won - der -

ful You are. (How pow - er - ful You are.)
ful You are. (How won - der - ful You are.)

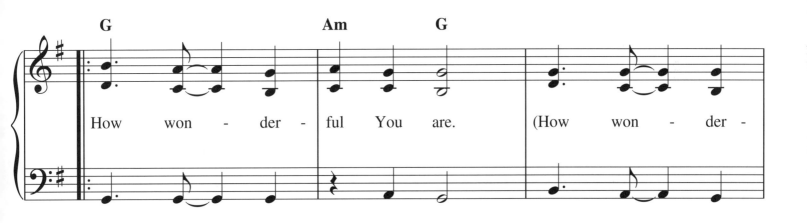

How won - der - ful You are. (How won - der -

ful Your are.) Hail, hail,___ Lion of Ju - dah!

1          8vb

# THERE IS NONE LIKE YOU

Words and Music by
LENNY LeBLANC

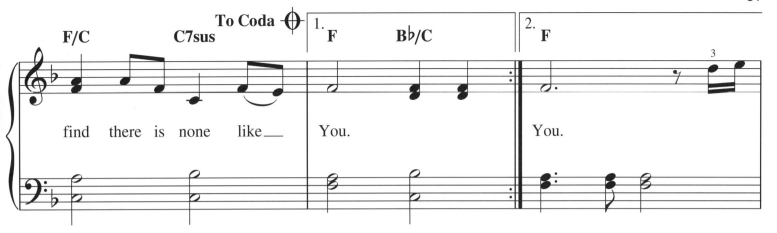

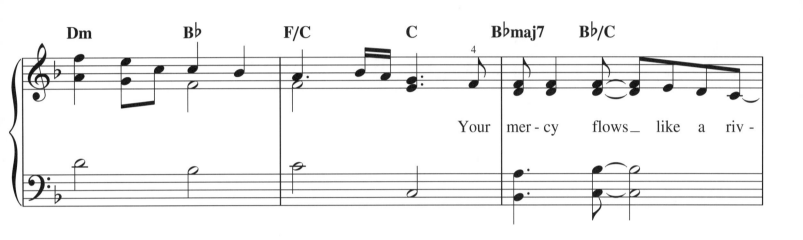

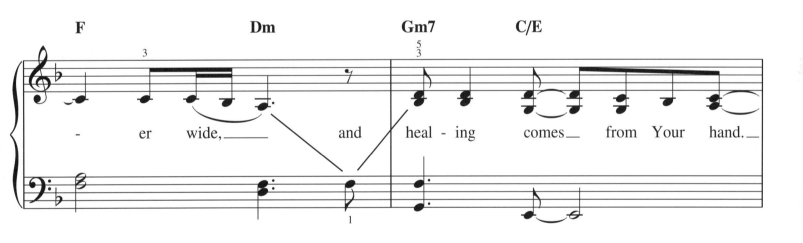

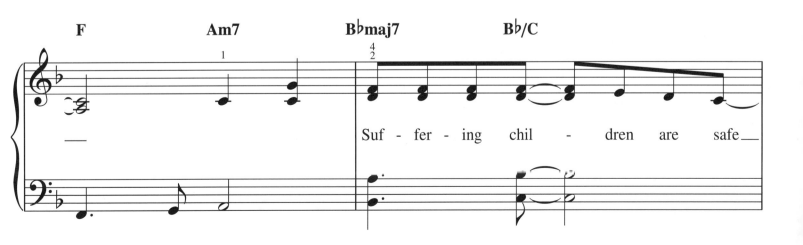

D.S. al Coda

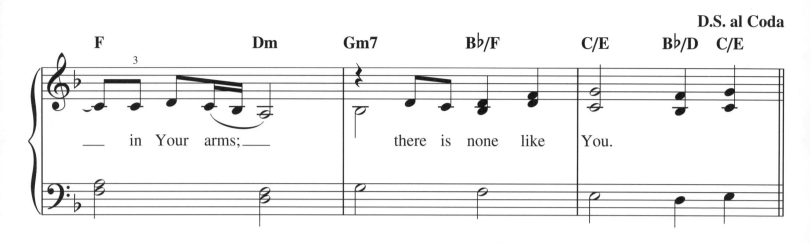

in Your arms;____ there is none like You.

**CODA**

You. There is none like____ You.

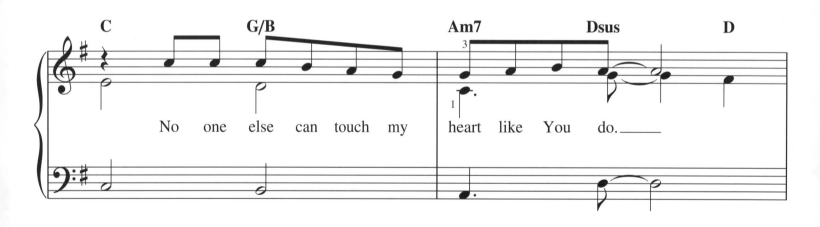

No one else can touch my heart like You do.____

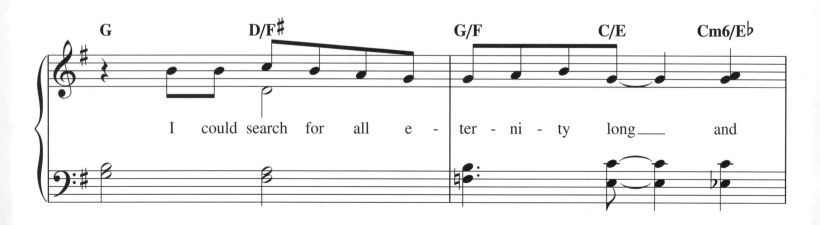

I could search for all e - ter - ni - ty long____ and

find there is none like&#95;&#95; You.

I could search for all e -

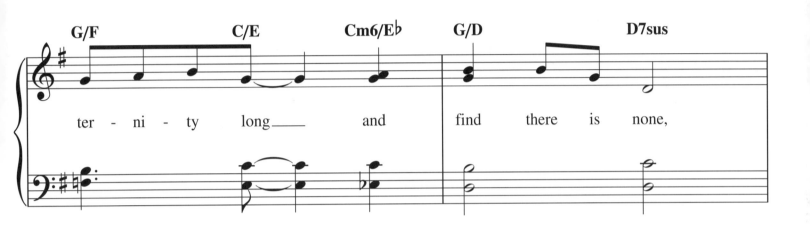

ter - ni - ty long&#95;&#95; and find there is none,

there is none, there is none like&#95;&#95; You.

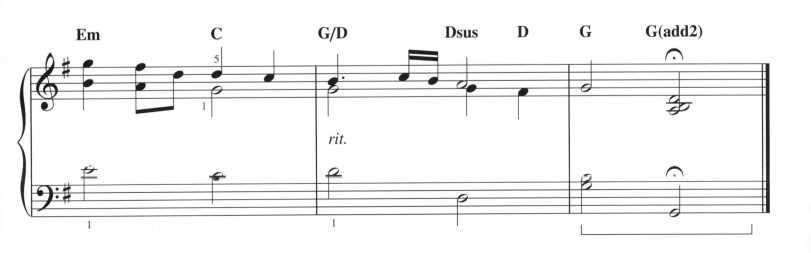

rit.

# WORTHY IS THE LAMB

Words and Music by
DARLENE ZSCHECH

**Worshipfully**

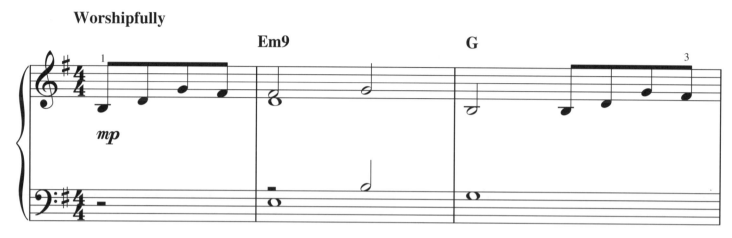

*With pedal*

Thank You for the cross, _____ Lord. _____

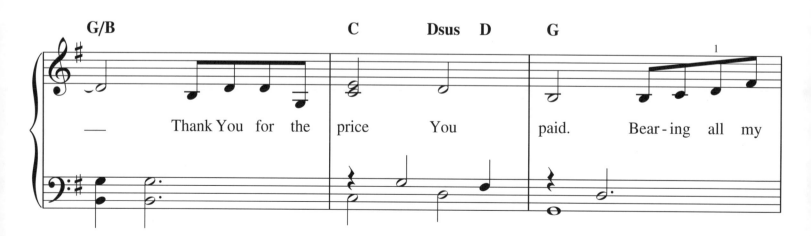

Thank You for the price You paid. Bear-ing all my

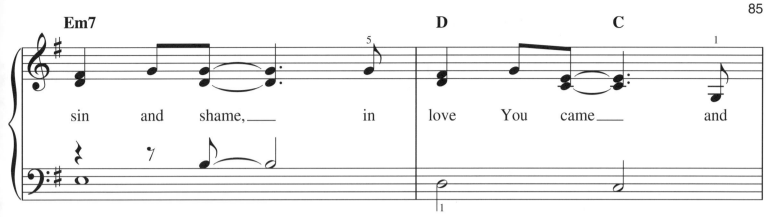

sin and shame,____ in love You came____ and

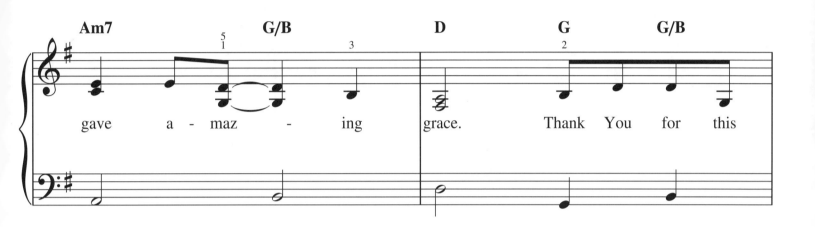

gave a - maz - ing grace. Thank You for this

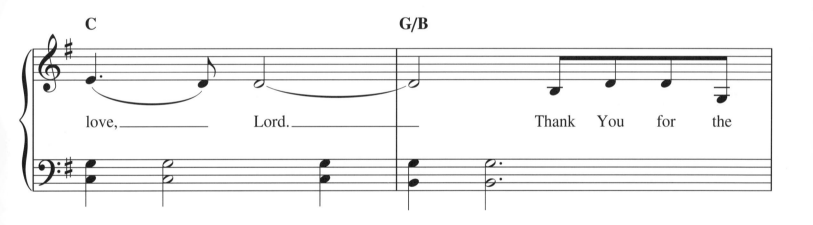

love,_____ Lord._____ Thank You for the

nail - pierced hands. Washed me in Your

cleans - ing flow,__ now all I know,__ Your for - give - ness and__ em -

brace. Wor - thy is__ the Lamb,

seat - ed on__ the throne. Crown You now__ with

man - y crowns,__ You reign vic - to - ri - ous.

High and lift - ed up,

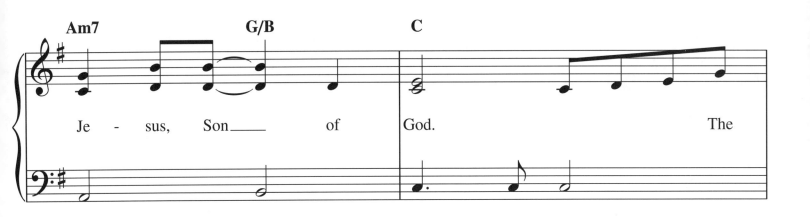

Je - sus, Son of God. The

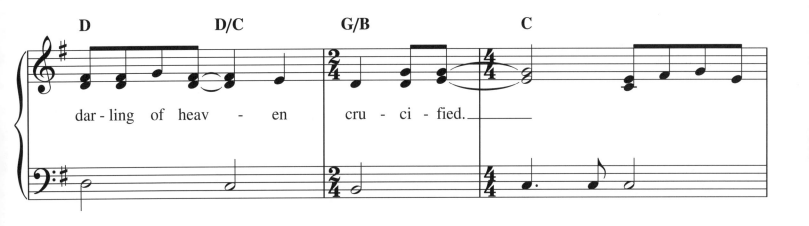

dar - ling of heav - en cru - ci - fied.

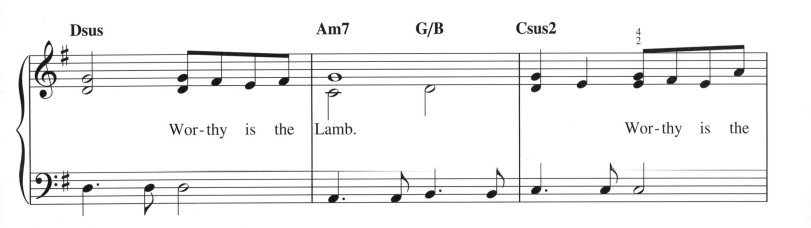

Wor - thy is the Lamb. Wor - thy is the

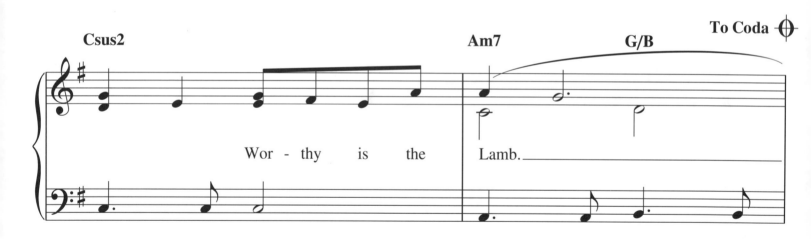

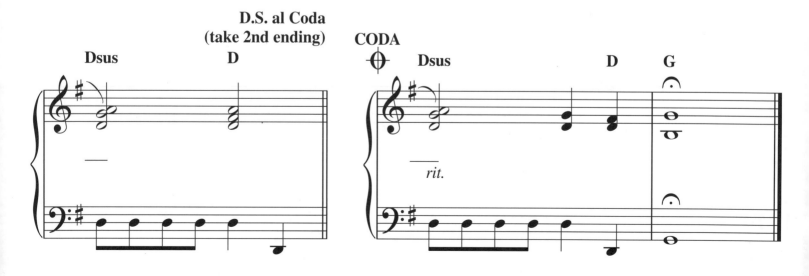